FALSE STARTS,
NEAR MISSES
AND
DANGEROUS
GOODS

FALSE STARTS, NEAR MISSES
AND
DANGEROUS GOODS

RAILWAYMEN'S STORIES
ABOUT THE CHALLENGES
OF RUNNING A RAILWAY

GEOFF BODY AND IAN BODY

The
History
Press

Arriva Train Wales unit 150230 runs into Platform 7 at Cardiff Central with a 'Valleys' service heading for Barry Island.

Cover illustration: A scene of locomotive neglect typical of many places with the coming of the end of steam.

First published 2017

The History Press
The Mill, Brimscombe Port
Stroud, Gloucestershire, GL5 2QG
www.thehistorypress.co.uk

British Library Cataloguing in Publication Data.
A catalogue record for this book is available from the British Library.

ISBN 978 0 7509 7027 3

Typesetting and origination by The History Press
Printed and bound by Imak, Turkey

CONTENTS

INTRODUCTION, SOURCES AND ACKNOWLEDGEMENTS

Transport is a highly complex business, nowhere more so than in its railway arm. Paradoxically, it is an industry that seeks constantly and earnestly to be routine and orderly but stands no chance of total and consistent achievement of that objective. There is no certainty in the day-to-day operation and the plan, however carefully organised, is always liable to interruption: an unexpected influx of passengers, mechanical breakdown, the vagaries of weather, the acts of trespassers and vandals – the possibilities are endless.

A great dividend from this uncertainty is that railwaymen are permanently schooled and ready to deal with the unexpected and challenging. Indeed, they have been doing so since the birth of the railway. It follows that significant incidents in a railwayman's career tend to be etched deeply in his memory and the aim of *False Starts, Near Misses and Dangerous Goods* has been to unearth a range of these recollections and put them together in a readable and entertaining form that also reveals something of the complexities of the railway business and how the industry is organised to manage them.

The writers between them have a good few, strong memories of their own, but this book could not have been prepared without the huge input from its contributors. Most of them are names that have appeared in the acknowledgements in previous books, and to everyone mentioned in the heading for each entry we are extremely grateful. To single out anyone would be an invidious task but, once again, Bryan Stone has done us proud from his photographic library, recalling in his present home in Switzerland the years when his wisdom resulted in a record of the detail of railway working that others had overlooked. New contributor David Barraclough has poured out a wealth of material from his time at Boston, Wath and Glasgow, and this book would not have happened without the efforts of long-term colleague and good friend Bill Parker. For inspiring contributions, his ideas, checking and much other help, thank you Bill.

As so often before, Amy Rigg and the editorial staff at The History Press have combined efficiency with unending helpfulness. Our thanks to them and the promotion, sales and other folk at The History Press.

Except where otherwise credited, the illustrations used in the book are all from the authors' collections.

The departure board at Basingstoke gives echoes of the past: Burford, Itchen Abbas, Torrington, Bideford, Lynton – stations long gone.

GLOSSARY

absolute block	standard railway signalling arrangement, ensuring only one train can be in a designated track section at a time
ASLEF	Associated Society of Locomotive Engineers and Firemen
bay platform	dead-end station platform
BG	Brake Gangwayed (guard's brake van/parcels van with bogie wheels)
bogie	the framework carrying wheels which, in turn, is fixed to the railway vehicle
bogie bolster wagon	long wheelbase flatbed freight vehicle
BR	British Rail
BRB	British Railways Board
BRSA	British Railways Staff Association
BSK	Brake Standard Corridor (second-class corridor passenger coach with brake section)
BT	British Transport
BTP	British Transport Police
catch points	a safety turnout designed to derail vehicles running back out of control
CIÉ	Córas Iompair Éireann (Irish Railways)
clamping/clipping and scotching	a clip and a wedge used to immobilise a set of points (often for engineering work)
conrail	conductor rail in direct current, third-rail electrified systems
CP	Canadian Pacific

demurrage	charge made to freight customers when wagons were not released within the stipulated period
DI	District Inspector, often seen as the key local 'rules and operations' expert
DOO	Driver Only Operation (no assistant in the driving cab)
DMU	diesel multiple unit
DTM	Divisional Traffic Manager
ECS	empty coaching stock (passenger vehicles running out of service)
EMU	electric multiple unit
facing and trailing points	facing points are divergent and allow a change of a train's direction, while trailing points are convergent
four foot	space between the two running rails
fully fitted	the existence of braking operated by the locomotive on all the vehicles in the train
GWR	Great Western Railway
hot axle-box	lack of lubricant on the axle-box, which can cause the metal to overheat and possibly fracture
hump	an incline from which shunted vehicles have a free run down into a marshalling yard or sidings
Hyfit	traditional open merchandise wagon with train-operated brakes
IO	Inspecting Officer
LDC	Local Departmental Committee (the basic unit of local staff representation)
lengthman	an engineer with responsibility for a specific 'length' of track
light engine	engine operating without any attached vehicles
Lowmac	a flat bogie freight vehicle with a lowered centre for extra height clearance
merry-go-round	freight service which unloads automatically while on the move
MoT	Ministry of Transport
off the road	a colloquial term for a derailment
out and home	a staff driving/guard shift involving out and back in the same day – relates to the days when overnight lodgings were not uncommon

partially fitted	includes some vehicles that only have handbrakes available
permanent way/p-way	traditional railway term for the track and supporting structure
permissive block	signalling system allowing for more than one train in a single section
pilotman	member of staff acting as the authority for a train to enter a signalling section
PNB	Physical Needs Break (guaranteed break in a turn of duty, initially between the third and fifth hour of work)
PRO	Public Relations Officer
right away	signal given to a driver to start the train
second man	additional assistant driver
seven bells	'stop and examine' signal sent from a signal box to the one ahead to stop the train because of a defect on it
slide chairs	the unit for holding a rail to a sleeper with the additional facility of accommodating movement where points are involved
SLW	Single-Line Working (two-directional train operation over a single set of rails)
SNCF	Société Nationale des Chemins de Fer Français (France's national state-owned railway company)
Special Traffic Notice	list of services that have been planned outside the standard regular timetable
sprag	a piece of wood put through the wheel spokes to prevent movement
switch and stock rails	stock rails are fixed while switches move to facilitate a change of direction
TA	Traffic Apprentice (long-running training scheme to fast-track individuals to senior management)
tail traffic	freight vehicles attached to a booked passenger service
ten foot	the central space on a four-track railway (which may not actually be 10ft)
Tipfit	fitted brake wagon designed to be unloaded by tipping
TOPS	Total Operations Processing System (a national system for managing the use of freight vehicles)
TPO	Travelling Post Office

track circuit	simple electrical device to detect the existence of a train on a particular stretch of track
trap points	similar to catch points but usually designed to divert vehicles into a sand trap
TSO	Tourist Standard Open (open second-class coach (non-corridor))
Up line and Down line	used to differentiate lines by the direction of travel and not related to inclines
vacuum brake	vehicle-braking system where the maintenance of a vacuum keeps the brakes off
Vanfit	brake-fitted box wagon
Weekly Traffic Notice	temporary advice of amendments to operations
wrong side failure	failure of a piece of equipment that compromises safety

A COUPLE OF NEAR MISSES

———◇———

Bill Parker was to encounter some new and rather unexpected experiences at one of his relief stationmaster postings

As a young, summer-relief stationmaster I spent most of one summer in the early 1950s covering the stationmaster's vacancy at Claypole, a small station in a rural area on the East Coast Main Line just south of Newark. Despite the few passenger trains stopping there, the passenger activity could be fairly busy, particularly in the mornings and evenings and on market days at Grantham and Newark. There were three sidings in the goods yard together with a cattle dock and a goods shed. Quite a few parcels were dealt with and there was some freight traffic, mainly agricultural and coal. It was a good station for gaining all-round experience.

I had visits from the district passenger manager and the assistant district operating superintendent, both of whom had been on the selection panel that had appointed me, and both giving me a thorough but encouraging grilling. The district inspector (DI) also made several visits and tested my signalling abilities by watching me work the signal box and the heavy, wheel-operated level-crossing gates. The district wagon inspector checked my daily wagon returns and the demurrage position in connection with the raising of charges for wagons not emptied within the stipulated free period.

One morning I was less than pleasantly surprised by a knock on my office door and the appearance of a tall, barrel-shaped, red-faced man in uniform who entered and announced, rather aggressively, 'I'm the sack inspector from Lincoln sack headquarters.' I was aware of letters I had received demanding 'sack returns', but the whole sack business was a mystery to me. At the time, the railway companies provided free grain sacks for the conveyance of corn by rail, but these were supposed to be accounted for and charges should have been raised for loss, damage or non-return within the free period allowed.

In my defence, I had eventually found and sent off some of the completed earlier returns when prompted by the third letter, but could find no book of regulations about sacks – most unusual, as there were regulations about everything on the railway – and my neighbouring stationmasters were less than helpful about what they considered a matter of minor importance. The more recent returns I had compiled using my mathematical skills, along with a measure of inventiveness. Now, however, nemesis had arrived and the inspector's visit was clearly to chastise me for the delays and check my recent submissions.

The gods must have been with me that day, for just before the serious interrogation started I had a telephone call from the signalman saying that there was a hot axle-box on one of the wagons of an up freight approaching Claypole. I had been 'saved by the bell' – in fact, the seven bells 'stop and examine' train signal. My inquisitor accepted that my priority now had to be dealing with the emergency on the main line.

I was soon occupied with the business of detaching the defective Vanfit wagon into our goods sidings and arranging for its freight sundries contents to be reloaded into an empty van that happened to be in the goods shed. By the time I returned to my office the sack inspector had gone, leaving a note saying that he 'would be back'. Fortunately by that time I had moved on to another appointment!

My time in this job involved an on–call responsibility, which required me to lodge locally on alternate weeks. My landlady was typical of her calling, with the house impeccably clean and myself hugely overfed, necessitating the lengthy bike rides to and from the station to help control my weight. Although I spent long hours at the station, especially working the signal box in the evenings, I needed other interesting activities.

The village cricket team, its supporters and the pavilion's bar were most welcoming; so, too, was the Anglican vicar and his church members, particularly the organist and choir. The latter told me how much they would like to sing anthems, many packets of which were stacked away in the vestry. I volunteered to help and instantly became acting choirmaster. Because the organist, a good bass singer, wanted to sing in the choir, I also became piano accompanist and sub-organist. The choir's enthusiasm and performance quality was wonderful, tackling, as they did so very competently, the choral music of Byrd, Bach, Handel, Stanford and Elgar.

I also enjoyed the choir's habitual adjournment to the pub after choir practice and Sunday services. There, unsurprisingly, they led the singing of

LNER 5317/9/45—6,000   G. 739

LONDON AND NORTH EASTERN RAILWAY.

GOODS DEPARTMENT.

....Station.

Telephone No......................

.... 194.....

Reference :

....

Dear Sir,

(1) On.................................194...., you

hired from this Station..........................

L.N.E.R. Sacks ....

which have not been returned here.

(2) M..

of ....

transfer.........................L.N.E.R. sacks to

you on and from..............................194.....

   Will you please complete the annexed
card showing how the sacks have been
disposed of, and return to me.

       Yours faithfully,

PENNY STAMP

PRINTED PAPER.

THE ADDRESS TO BE WRITTEN ON THIS SIDE.

REPLY.

LONDON & NORTH EASTERN RAILWAY.

GOODS DEPARTMENT.

The availability of sacks for hire influenced many grain forwardings to rail, but getting the sacks back was another matter, despite the use of this form.

rather less religious songs, along with the other locals. As I played the piano, I had the benefit of free beer!

The choir members were a very friendly group, revealed in one way for which I was quite unprepared. After one practice a sturdy, well-proportioned and attractive soprano took hold of my hands, complimented me on my playing skills and forthwith propositioned me! How does a young relief stationmaster react to something like this? There was nothing about it in the railway rule book, nor in the advice my stationmaster father had given me. Completely overwhelmed, way beyond surprised, I spluttered out, 'Sorry, but I have to go back to the station to do the sack returns.' Perhaps the young lady had talents other than her singing ones – I would never know – but I did try to avoid eye contact during the remainder of my time conducting the choir and had learned something for my many subsequent years of musical activities. It was, at least, a rare occasion when sack returns had come in useful!

WHAT'S ON NEXT WEEK?

————◁◦▷————

Jim Dorward describes the variety of content appearing in a typical
British Rail Special Traffic Notice

British Rail's (BR) ability to move different types of special-passenger train traffic over its extensive pre-Beeching network in the 1960s is well illustrated by the diversity of trains listed in almost any Weekly Traffic Notice of the time. For example, the Scottish Region's SC2 Notice for Saturday 6 to Friday 12 June 1964 included the following:

Saturday 6 June

Llandovery to Glasgow (Central) and Edinburgh (Princes Street)
A military special. Such trains were easily recognised by the ratio of first- and second-class seats provided. This train had thirteen firsts for officers and 265 seconds for soldiers. The train split at Carstairs, the front portion continuing to Glasgow (Central) and the rear portion changing direction for the journey to the soon-to-be-closed Edinburgh (Princes Street).

London (St Pancras) (5 June) to Oban and Return
A 'hotel on wheels'. This thirteen-coach special, including sleeping and restaurant cars, was carrying passengers for a boat trip to Staffa and Iona. The train was booked to arrive at Oban at 8 a.m. and depart for the journey back to London at 8.55 p.m. The route included the now-closed line between Dunblane and Crianlarich. The trip would involve some beautiful scenery, provided BR had arranged for there to be no rain in the notoriously wet area around Oban.

Irvine to Kilmarnock
This was a 'Tote' special comprising a single BG bogie brake and parcels vehicle for the conveyance of Tote betting equipment used at a nearby race meeting. The vehicle was subsequently to be attached at Kilmarnock to the regular 9.25 p.m. Glasgow (St Enoch) to London (St Pancras) service. The operators of the equipment would have been amazed at today's Internet betting.

Scottish Region
Special Traffic
Notice, June 1964.
(Jim Dorward)

PRIVATE and not for publication   No. 23

BRITISH RAILWAYS
SCOTTISH REGION

SPECIAL
TRAFFIC NOTICE

Sc.2

SATURDAY, 6th JUNE

TO

FRIDAY, 12th JUNE, 1964

EXPLANATION OF REFERENCES.

The references appearing in the Working Time Tables are applicable plus the following:—

Adexc—Advertised day excursion.
Evex—Evening excursion.
Garex—Guaranteed excursion.
Halfex—Half-day excursion.
K—Refreshments.

PR—Prepal.
Parspec—Unadvertised Party Special.
T—Stops for ticket examination or collection only.
Z—Lavatory purposes.

GLASGOW & SOUTH WEST DIVISION,   J. G. URQUHART,
GLASGOW   Divisional Manager

Renfrew (Fulbar Street) to Stevenston and Return

Sunday school picnic. The interesting aspect of this train was the arrangement that BR had to make for the train to travel over the goods line between Paisley (Abercorn) and Paisley Goods. This needed the introduction of Absolute Block Signalling Regulations, a 10mph speed restriction and the clamping and scotching of facing points. One wonders if the revenue managed to cover the permanent-way men's overtime!

Saturday 6 and Sunday 7 June

Bertam Mills Circus

Two special trains from Workington to Stranraer Harbour along the now-closed line between Dumfries and Stranraer. Bertram Mills Circus had used

17

four special trains for many years to move the circus from town to town. By 1964, however, television had started to change the live entertainment world. Consequently, prior to closing down the tenting show, Bertram Mills had decided to have a tour of Ireland using only two BR trains for the journey from Workington to Stranraer Harbour and the return journey to Ascot (West) where they had their winter quarters. Two special trains were assembled by the Irish railways.

The 9 p.m. from Workington included two passenger coaches and eleven bogie bolster wagons loaded with circus trailers. Speed was restricted to 25mph. The 12.10 a.m. (Sunday) from Workington conveyed four passenger coaches, elephants and horses. Speed was restricted to 30mph. These trains, particularly the one with the circus trailers, brought to an end the close working relationship between BR and Bertram Mills, together with the possibility of free tickets for some of the BR staff involved.

Tuesday 9 June

Perth to Gourock and Return
Two specials for a sail on the River Clyde for the General Accident Insurance Company's annual staff outing. Both trains included restaurant cars and the timings were designed to give passengers adequate time to enjoy the delights of a BR four-course lunch and high tea.

Wednesday 10 June

Glasgow (St Enoch) to Greenock (Princes Pier)
This was a special train for Scots immigrating to Canada on Canadian Pacific Railway's *Empress of England*. A special parcels train preceded the passenger train, conveying luggage and mails for the transatlantic crossing. No doubt many a tear was shed on the platform at St Enoch station.

There is little wonder that when the Special Traffic Notice arrived each week signalmen would say, 'What's on next week … and is there any overtime?'

Central
Scotland lines.
(Jim Dorward)

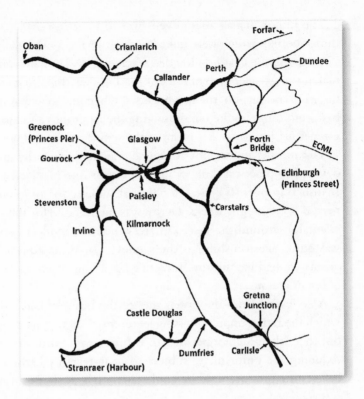

COURSE FARE

————— ◄o► —————

Geoff Body was privileged to attend several BR courses, acquiring
a few unusual memories in the process

BR ran a great many instructive courses, chief among them a trio aimed at
junior, middle and senior management. The aim of a good course is clearly
to imbue knowledge that gets ingrained in life and work skills, but a good
course will also create sufficient liveliness to result in a few extra curricular
and memorable incidents. Or so I found it on these three particular courses.

The junior management event was so long ago that I recall only two things, both of which were linked to the catering. One is that the venue was a country house near London that was being used to train young chefs – and making an excellent job of it if our food was anything to go by. The other is the embarrassment of the first breakfast when my polite passing of the sugar basin and tongs resulted in dislodging the latter into a full jug of milk with a generous, impromptu baptism of the senior officer sitting nearby.

The middle management course was held at Derby and was largely devoted to practical skills, while the senior one involved a period in the British Transport (BT) Staff College at Woking for an intense instruction period lasting eight weeks. Derby was memorable for the end-of-course excursion around the Peak District when the rendering of rugby songs was quite as astonishing as the scenery was beautiful. At both of these events we had lectures on 'Effective Speaking', each memorable, but for different reasons.

A colleague from the hotels side of the business had a slight stammer, which the rather unprepossessing lecturer set out to remedy in what turned out to be the cruellest performance I have ever witnessed. It consisted of reducing the unfortunate subject to near-tears by barbed criticism and devastating pressure until he could barely talk at all. But it worked; a cure was achieved.

The other presenter on the art of effective speaking was an attractive woman in her late twenties or early thirties, very well groomed and confident. This was a challenge that one red-blooded member of the course could not resist. He had a slight hair lip, which tinged his speech, although not to any great degree. Referring to this, he stood and asked the lecturer if she could help with a remedy, clearly ready to delight in her failure to meet his challenge.

She was more than his match. 'Mr X,' she said, 'if your question is a serious one I presume you will be willing to act upon any advice I give you.'

Already the challenger was snared. If he said no it made a mockery of posing the question. If he said yes she could impose pretty well whatever demeaning action she liked upon him, and duly did so when he had to indicate assent.

'Thank you, Mr X. What I want you to do is stand in front of a mirror each morning and evening, put a finger on the damaged lip and splutter at least ten times. And I'd like you to do it for the whole of the remainder of the course, and in front of your colleagues as an earnest of your good faith.'

The lecturer's would-be tormentor had been well bested and took it well. We warmed to our speaker and what she then had to pass on in her lecture.

The Woking course was no sinecure; the reading list alone would have occupied the rest of my days. But there were several consolations, not least a croquet court where I acquired a little skill and a lot of respect for an intriguing and sometimes vicious game. The principal beat me in the prestigious final, so, along with a mathematics wizard from the British Railways Board (BRB) headquarters, we turned to beating the odds on the fruit machine in the relaxation room. He was a random-numbers expert and we did manage to make a profit, but the grand total of 19d per 2 hours of effort was not generally adjudged overly impressive.

A feature of each Woking course was a short visit to some out-based activities, in our case to the Continent to marvel at the then-new Schiphol Airport in Amsterdam and the pioneer activities of a haulier specialising in the handling of garments on racks. From our visit to the former we had

Croquet interval for British Transport Staff College course No. 16 with Louis Verberckt threatening to go home to Belgium following defeat!

The traditional course group photograph where we posed in front of the British Transport Staff College at Woking, with the principal and his staff in the front row.

to use a tram to get back to our hotel and, for some obscure reason, were moved to collective song to lighten the journey. Getting rather carried away with the occasion, we were so encouraged by our fellow tram passengers' applause that we went round the tram circuit again, still in full voice. What a contrast was our return journey early on the final morning of the trip when the temptations of duty-free Geneva on board the BR ferry had taken its toll. The stooping, ashen-faced gang that disembarked at Harwich looked as little like a group of potential high flyers as did the bollards to which our vessel was moored!

We had recovered by the time of the end-of-course show that, by tradition, the members staged. In drag, with awful songs and rhymes, we produced our version of 'The Woking Ladies Finishing School' and a sketch in which we parodied the assessment process by a, hopefully, witty critique of the staff and tutors who had served us so well but with no light hand.

DRAMA AT CHESTER

From his time as area manager at Chester, Peter Whittaker recalls
two serious accidents

Tattenhall Junction, 1971

It was a lovely summer evening early in July and I had been in my first real management job, as area manager at Chester, for just four months. I was mowing the lawn prior to taking the family – my wife and three very young boys – on holiday the next morning. Midway through my task my wife appeared to tell me that Chester Control was on the phone. This was unusual, as I was not on call, but they thought I might like to know there had been a serious derailment on the patch.

This advice arrived some 2 hours after the actual incident, so, rather than add my presence to the undoubtedly already overcrowded accident site, I went straight to Chester Control to brief myself, having told my long-suffering wife to continue the holiday packing, with no expectation of when I might return home. On arrival, the story I found was that a returning schools party special train from Rhyl to Smethwick had become derailed on buckled rails at Tattenhall Junction outside Chester, with serious casualties and at least one fatality.

I was able to establish that the emergency services had been on site very rapidly and were performing extremely well. I also contacted my deputy at the site to check that my presence there was not needed at that stage and then got in touch with Birmingham Control. The power of the network again – in charge at the Birmingham end was a friend and former colleague, Peter Barlow. He had managed to obtain from the school a list of the children, teachers and other adults who had been on the trip. I was gradually able to assemble, by contacts with the crash site, the police and the local hospitals, a list of the survivors who were returning to Birmingham, those awaiting collection by parents and others, and casualties who had been taken to hospitals at Chester or Wrexham.

For several hours it was hoped that there might be only one fatality but, sadly, as the last of the wrecked coaches was being examined, a second, unidentifiable body was discovered. By comparing my list with Peter's we were able to establish that an 11-year-old boy was missing, later identified.

It is difficult to imagine the horror entailed in this situation of setting out from a deprived area of Birmingham for a sunny day at the seaside and then to find the party ended in such a way. The strength of feeling among the Chester staff was such that on my return from holiday I discovered they had raised a spontaneous cash collection for the school. The gesture and the amount raised were such that I felt I must deliver it personally to Benson Road school rather than just send a cheque by post. The walk from Smethwick Rolfe Street station through Winson Green to the school caused me to reflect again upon the responsibility we carry as transport operators.

Chester Station, 1972

On a Tuesday evening in early May, after a particularly stretching day as area manager, Chester Control came on the phone at 9 p.m. I was not on call and so only likely to be contacted about something fairly serious. A voice said, 'Sir, there has been a serious accident at the station and the station roof is on fire.'

As I stopped at traffic lights approaching the outskirts of Chester, the whole sky seemed to be alight, reminding me of my earliest childhood memory of a wartime bombing raid on Liverpool. I thought, 'This is not just the station roof – it must be the whole station on fire!'

On arrival at Chester station I was greeted by not only a raging fire but a scene of general destruction. A freight train from Ellesmere Port to Mold Junction had run away down the falling gradient approaching Chester and run through points set for the bay platform, colliding there with an empty diesel multiple unit (DMU) at about 20mph. The first coach of the DMU was completely destroyed and the second coach was torn from its bogies and thrown up on to the adjacent platform where it came to rest having demolished half of the refreshment room.

A major fire had started when the burst fuel tanks of both the DMU and the freight locomotive ignited – it had indeed set the station roof on fire. There were additional complications: the first five wagons of the freight train were tank wagons containing kerosene, petrol and gas oil. Petrol from two of these tanks had begun to boil and been forced out of the pressure-relief valves, adding to the conflagration.

Fortunately, the fire brigade was based locally and had arrived at the scene very quickly, but they were faced with a challenging situation. Mercifully and, in the circumstances, miraculously, there were no serious injuries. My duty manager had performed magnificently. Having established that all emergency precautions had been taken, he then very quickly – and at no small risk to himself – uncoupled the freight train between the third and fourth tank wagons, averting a further extension of the fire. Under my direction he then used the same shunting locomotive to further remove some other tank wagons from an adjacent siding. These contained ethylene dibromide which, when heated, can discharge some highly toxic gases.

By using copious amounts of foam and continuously spraying the tank wagons to control the temperature inside, the fire brigade was able to contain the fire, although it was not finally extinguished for some 4 hours. The senior fire officer on site advised me that the fire was out and he was on his way home. I asked whether this meant that my staff could get into the area and start some sort of a clear up. He confirmed that this would be fine but, fortunately, some sixth sense sent me in search of his deputy, who was appalled at the idea. The tank wagons would need to be sprayed continuously for at least another 8 hours before the site could be declared free of further risk – an interesting lesson in seeking a second opinion, even in the case of experts! When I asked later what would have happened if they had been unable to cool the tanks sufficiently, the answer was that there would have been a fireball over the whole of Chester.

REPRIEVE

————◁○▷————

Philip Benham recalls the case of an unusual solution which had been applied to a pigeon problem at Scarborough

Like most businesses, BR had tight procedures to guard against fraud and financial impropriety. Wherever cash was involved everything had to be properly recorded with documented evidence to explain every item of expenditure. Thus, one of my jobs as area manager at York was to 'sign off' disbursements where petty cash had been used to pay for small items. These could range from the purchase of stamps for correspondence through to taxis provided for passengers who had missed train connections. One of the most fanciful explanations I recall for a particular payment was 'wages for rodent operative' – this was actually milk for the station cat.

More serious, however, was an item in the monthly return from Scarborough booking office simply described as 'purchase of new gun'. 'What gun?' I asked in an urgent call to the station manager. He was as surprised as I was, but promised to investigate.

A day later, back came the explanation. Scarborough station had, and still has, a train shed covering the main platforms, with the rafters offering ideal roosting sites for pigeons. While great for the pigeons, the experience for passengers below was rather less pleasant when the pigeons did what pigeons do! To get round the problem, the station supervisor had found a way to tackle the difficulty with regular Saturday-night pigeon shoots. For this purpose he had commandeered a family heirloom in the form of a First World War rifle. Sadly, after more than half a century, the rifle had fired its last round, so a replacement had been bought.

There was a fundamental problem with all this. No firearms certificate could be found for either the old rifle or its replacement, quite apart from the unacceptable practice of uncontrolled use of a gun in a railway station. Of course, the problem of pigeons in railway buildings was not new, and there were other less dramatic ways to try to control them. For now, though, the pigeons of Scarborough would sleep more easily on a Saturday night.

26

STRIKE SERVICE

————◁○▷————

In the difficult period of a train drivers' strike, Philip Benham and
Nottingham-area colleagues kept many services going

The early 1980s were difficult times for industrial relations, with the still
relatively new government of Prime Minister Margaret Thatcher determined
to change the rules. The steel industry had only recently seen a major strike
and trouble was brewing in the coal mines, while the BRB was striving
to improve operational efficiency against a background of much, often ill
founded, criticism for being out of date.

The year 1982 was to prove a particularly challenging one. The issue at
stake was the lengths of duty that train crews should work, with the BRB
wanting to move away from a rigid 8-hour day to more flexible shifts of
between 6 and 10 hours. After months of threatened action, the National
Union of Railwaymen went on strike in late June, but returned to work after
just two days. The Associated Society of Locomotive Engineers and Firemen
(ASLEF [the drivers' union]) then called an all-out strike from early July.

I was the on-call officer for the Nottingham division on the day the
strike was due to start (Sunday 4 July). Early in the afternoon indications
started to come through to the control office that some drivers, particularly
at the Leicester depot, were prepared to continue work as normal. This was
encouraging, but the work of one depot tended to be closely integrated with
those from another – a train worked by a driver from depot A would often
be handed over to another from depot B at a station en route – so how could
we make the best use of those drivers who were prepared to work?

I made my way to the control office and, with the help of the deputy
chief controller and head of the division's trains office, we devised a plan.
To understand our approach, a little explanation is needed about crew
diagrams. These diagrams set out what each driver, second man or guard has
to do during their shift. For each turn of duty, the following details are given:
sign-on and sign-off times; allowances for preparing engines or stock; starting
and finishing points for each train worked; which turn they are relieved by;
and times for meal or physical needs breaks (PNB), which then had to allow
30 minutes clear somewhere between the third and fifth hours after signing on.

Apart from local shunting and trip working, the divisions rarely became involved in producing crew diagrams. On the London Midland Region they were normally issued by the train planning office in Crewe and were subject to consultation with trade union representatives. Tearing them up and starting again just did not happen, but in order to produce a coherent train plan that is exactly what we did. New diagrams were drawn up to get the maximum use 'out and back' from those drivers expected to report for work. In particular, we made sure times were built in for a PNB and avoided handovers from a driver at one depot to another who might be on strike. We figured, correctly, that if a driver had made the decision to work he would be prepared to accept new diagrams.

Initially, we concentrated on preparing new diagrams to support an emergency passenger timetable, and, to make life simple, planned to use only DMUs, as these worked single-manned. The strategy worked well, and for the first full day of the strike on the Monday we were able to offer a regular-frequency DMU service between Derby, Nottingham and Leicester that was rather better than normal! Venturing further afield was more challenging but by Tuesday, as the full availability of drivers at Leicester became clear, it proved possible to reintroduce loco-hauled services on Midland Main Line services through to London St Pancras. Soon, a few drivers from other depots indicated they wanted to work, including Cambridge Street in London, enabling services to be extended north to Sheffield. By now we were able to find enough crews to offer a timetable approaching normality on the Midland Main Line, although little was running on the cross country and secondary routes to the likes of Birmingham, Lincoln, Peterborough or Crewe.

Elsewhere in the division, it was proving possible to move some vital coal services to power stations and aggregate trains from the quarries at Mountsorrel and around Coalville. By the second week of the strike it was evident that sympathy from depots across the country was starting to ebb away, although many depots remained solid in their support to the end.

After a fortnight, following the intervention of the TUC, ASLEF called off the action. In the event, there was a compromise on the length of rosters, with the final outcome being turn-of-duty lengths of between 7 and 9 hours, somewhat less than BRB had intended.

It had by no means been plain sailing. Industrial disputes are always very emotive and the actions of the working drivers had, of course, been highly unpopular with those on strike. Picket lines had been set up, including one on the ring-road overbridge south of Derby that was prominently in the

No. 45104 with an eight-coach strike 'special' passing the idle Freightliner depot at Beeston, Nottingham. (Philip Benham)

line of vision for drivers of passing trains. Attempts to get the police to move the pickets on, or at least dismantle some of the more inflammatory placards, had little success.

So while there was satisfaction at having kept the trains moving, it was sad to see the bitterness that arose between good railwaymen – bitterness that may have lasted to the present day. One irony was that Leicester, the depot that decided to work, lost most of its London turns shortly afterwards with the introduction of High Speed Trains on the Midland Main Line. Personally, while understanding the logic, I felt this was a shame. Whatever the politics, as professional railway managers our job was to try to operate as good and as safe a service for passengers and freight customers as possible. That, I felt, we had done and, in the process, had helped our industry through a very dark time.

OFF THE ROAD – AGAIN

————◄○►————

During the course of a wide and varied railway career Bryan Stone
found himself derailed on quite a few occasions

Many of us at one time or another had duty call-outs to derailments. It was, however, my misfortune to be personally involved in several, although, as far as I know, I was never personally to blame. The following stories may seem trivial but be careful: in many walks of life, but especially on the railway, no mistake is trivial. A short distance from you someone else may also be making a trivial mistake and between the two of you it might end up in disaster. The railway, with its fixed systems, lends itself to safe operations, but these same systems mean that interdependencies are everywhere.

The first of my misfortunes was, as so often, a narrow escape. It was during National Service for the army at Longmoor on the Royal Engineers' military railway. I had passed various operators' trade tests and in spring 1961 was called to act as brakesman/shunter (guard, in BR language) on a specially ordered freight working from Longmoor Downs towards Liss. My workplace was a heavy 20-ton brake van, a bit like a big LNER Queen Mary; all was straightforward. I gave the 'right away' signal and the driver, who was a few wagon lengths ahead, acknowledged my wave from my platform and his steam WD 0-6-0ST responded briskly to the sharply opened regulator. We were off with vigour up the bank to Liphook Road and No. 6 bridge. Now, out of Longmoor Downs, the line climbed in a sharp curve, and just as I got back inside my van and shut the door there was a fierce jolt and an unholy bang. The brake van leapt into the air and came down again, with me close behind. We were now running quite fast and as I looked back there was a great red dust cloud over the single track, just clearing in the wind. But we were away and all seemed well; the van ran smoothly and there was no sign of an obstacle or damage, so, more shaken than convinced, I sat down. In a minute or two we were across No. 6 bridge and up at Weavers Down where I could signal the driver to stop.

There I climbed down, told the blockman (signalman) to refuse other trains, told the driver what I was doing and went to examine the van. The rear wheels of the two-axle van were visibly scoured on the outside, the metal tyres brilliantly clean. That meant trouble. All I could think of was that the locomotive had spread the track, so that one rail was so loose in its spikes it had allowed the brake van to slip down between the rails. Then, improbable as it seemed, the van must have been lifted up and re-railed by the resilience of the following rails which were better secured. The more secure rails forced the wheels to jump back on to the track. My van had thus fallen into a 'hole' and then re-railed itself. By this time I was shaking, but we still had to examine the locomotive and train. Nothing seemed amiss and, unsurprisingly, the engine driver expressed thoughtful scepticism.

The blockman reported to Control, trains were stopped in that section, I signed the book and we completed our errand. On the way back, we were allowed down the line again. We disposed of our little train and the van in Longmoor yard, at which point I was told that I was needed, which was always bad news, but it was to hear that my report had allowed the location to be identified in time. The spikes of one rail had indeed been torn out and the rail had sprung open as we passed, widening the gauge. My heavy van had a long, fixed wheelbase and was perhaps most vulnerable, but the missing spikes had been hammered back home before our return and no more damage had been done. So I was, on balance, in favour, but the locomotive driver was cautioned for his zeal. That evening I walked up to see the spot. Sure enough, corresponding to my van's wheels, both rails had been equally scoured to a bright shine on the inside where the wheels had fallen down. I had a tale to tell, which I never forgot, but it could have ended very differently – we might have been off the road and down the bank – it was a narrow escape!

At Longmoor we had a lot of derailments, many of which were deliberate and for training purposes, which we had to set up for trainees and reservists to clear up. However, some were not deliberate; the year before I went to Longmoor, six sappers (Royal Engineers' soldiers) were killed in a disastrous collision involving a works train.

My next real derailment caught me out badly. In the summer of 1961, I was once again rostered for duty as brakesman/shunter – this time in a ramshackle old brake van, perhaps of London Midland and Scottish (LMS) origin, with an 0-6-0ST attached to my short extra goods – to pull out of the yard and cross the main road to Longmoor Downs. All was ready and I gave the hand signal from the top step to pull away. We didn't get far. Under the first bridge, as I leaned out holding the handrail, my van dropped off the road; my footstep did not hold and I fell sharply and mercifully away from the van. The engine driver saw me scramble to my feet to give the stop signal, with both hands raised. That was a wonder, since I had fallen on my outstretched right arm and, as was later discovered, the radius head in the elbow had snapped off; I could no longer move it.

This was the end of my Longmoor career. Being near demob day I spent the remainder of my service in hospital and in convalescence. I was, however, listed on Orders as 'on duty and not to blame'. My reputation was safe, but for over fifty years I have had a crooked and slightly shorter right arm.

So, in September 1961, I went to BR. After surviving my training, medical and various trials, I was posted to Doncaster division and, in 1965, was given a project in Grimsby. Passenger trains on the line from Doncaster to Grimsby were at that time rare and irregular, so this was a difficult posting. I needed to study the operational working at different times, so in the evening I took a lift home on a freight, of which there were many, and I had a duty pass. Conveniently it was a fast freight, 8.42 p.m. from Grimsby East Marsh to Doncaster Decoy, vacuum-braked on all wagons, which took the route through Brigg and Lincoln and then the Joint Line to Doncaster; power was usually a Brush 2750hp Type 4, later known as Class 47.

On 19 February 1965 I rode back on the almost new D1770 (built in October 1964), which played with its forty-five wagons (equal to fifty-nine in the jargon of the day, perhaps 600 tons). All went well and we duly rolled slowly into the Down Decoy yard on an arrival road.

As we stopped in the darkness by the lever-frame cabin, the shunter came up and uncoupled the engine from the train to release it to the Doncaster shed across the Great Northern Main Line. We didn't make it. I have forgotten the layout in detail, but we were then called forward, ready to stop and set back on another road; here, disaster took over – we eased forward, but obviously not far enough. The decisive set of points was between the two bogies. Setting back, the locomotive took two diverging tracks as far as it could and then dropped. It seemed an age as the cab settled, some 20 degrees from vertical, and I distinctly remember the driver saying, 'That's it: we're back on old England.' He then shut everything down.

After we had compared notes, reported and signed the book, I was free to go home. That meant a long walk over running lines to where my bicycle waited by the engine shed and a 6-mile ride home. The next day there was a short inquiry and I learned that D1770 was recovered in the night, unserviceable and damaged underneath. I never saw her again, but I know she became 47 175, and later still 47 575.

Now a big jump in time. In 1969 BR sent me to work at Intercontainer, the European rail company for international container traffic, located in Basel, Switzerland. There I travelled widely, including frequent trips to the USA. After 1994, when Intercontainer was being wound up, I was, for some years, a consultant expert on intermodal affairs and the USA trips became a big part of my work, but there was still time to relax a little. So on 16 May 1998 my wife and I, staying with old friends in Santa Fe, were on the first train of the season at Chama, New Mexico, to ride the Cumbres and Toltec 3ft gauge line to Osier and back – an all-day trip. Nos 489 and 497 (two 2-8-2s) took about twelve cars, roughly 500 tons, on a line with a 1 in 25 grade reaching 10,015ft (about 3,000m) altitude; snow lay deeply on the mountainsides. On the return trip, K27 Class 2-8-2, No. 463 (built in 1903) was used. As she was rounding a curve on the falling grade at a gentle 10mph, just 8 miles from home, a severe shock went through the train and we abruptly stopped. I said to my wife, 'We're off the road,' which she found incredible, as no one had noticed. I walked forward over the open platforms and, sure enough, there were the broken sleepers and spikes which showed that wheels had hit them hard. Old 463 was lying slightly out of line but upright, with most wheels off.

The engineer (driver) who had talked with me earlier said that the melting snow had undermined a well-known soft spot. Now, these are not toy trains: 463 weighs – engine and tender – just over 100 tons and the ramps that these engines carry had no effect, so another 2-8-2 came up from Chama with the tool vans.

Some 200ft above us, up the mountainside, was the highway. The brakesmen/conductors told us all (some 250 people) to walk up the mountainside, if we could, or walk a mile down the track to where the highway crossed the line. After a couple of hours we were rescued by private vehicles, SUVs and the Chama school bus. My wife and I were very late for dinner with our friends in Santa Fe – still an 80-mile drive further south.

There was, however, a sequel to this saga. Twelve years later, on 28 August 2010, I was a volunteer conductor with La Traction, which runs two Mallet steam locomotives in western Switzerland on the Chemins de Fer du Jura. On that particular day the train was a charter for US rail fans with both our engines. One of the group had a wind jacket with 'Cumbres and Toltec' printed across the back. This was too good to miss, so I spoke to him about my adventure in 1998. He was astonished and delighted and explained that he had been head brakesman on train 463, it had been badly damaged and they didn't get back to Chama until 2 a.m. We exchanged a lot of tales and I got him on to the footplate of our Mallet No. 206.

So railways have truly surrounded my long life, but I wasn't done yet. My wife Johanna comes from Lingen in Niedersachsen, Germany, where there is a nearby first-rate museum of the turf-cutting industry, which we visited in the autumn of 2013. At the museum there is a 600mm-gauge *Feldbahn* (a very light railway), which once brought turf to the dryers, and runs through the museum grounds; we of course took the 20-minute ride for €2. The trains consist of a diesel tractor and a number of light trolley cars.

Now, I do have some expectations – railways may go up and down and round corners, but it is usual for the rails to be at least reasonably parallel. This quality, however, seemed not to trouble the turf diggers. Nevertheless, speeds were low and we set off in high spirits – after all, I was a professional and understand these things. But guess what? After 15 minutes there was a severe jerk and we came to a sudden stop, as a wagon in the middle of the train was on the ground. Everyone got off and, using a large yellow jack that was found under the seat, there was some vigorous winding and a heave with the shoulder. We were ready to go again. The ride was happily completed but my reputation for being able to identify poor-quality track, especially with my wife's sister, is now severely in doubt.

We were often reminded how fine the line was between walking away and real trouble. Most of us railway professionals saw dreadful things at some time, and rules and equipment needed constant vigilance, but these stories might amuse even if – fifty-four years later in my Swiss village – I still have a crooked arm as a reminder.

NOCTURNE AT HAYMARKET

————◄○►————

Harry Knox describes a musical escapade performed by the young
cleaners at Haymarket Motive Power Depot

In the early part of my railway career, I spent some very happy years as a
cleaner/fireman at Edinburgh Haymarket Motive Power Depot. There, in
the late 1950s, was a large allocation of engine cleaners, most of whom,
myself included, were also employed on firing duties on a fairly regular
basis (and later continuously) from April through to October. During the
winter months, however, the cleaning squads were large, with some thirty-
five cleaners on three shifts spread over 24 hours, with no firing duties to
relieve the monotony.

With such a gathering of young men together, and there being little joy in
cleaning engines during the hours of darkness, there was, on the night shift,
often some nonsense or other being acted out. Mostly this was nothing more
than innocent fun but sometimes this 'fun' was taken to extremes. Whilst not
a paragon of innocence myself – but with an earnest desire to continue in
my chosen career – I have to say that, this time, common sense dictated that
one should not get involved in some of the wilder escapades, and thus I shied
clear of much of the nonsense.

Now to the story! Immediately south of the shed and bordering the
quadrupled main lines – the South Main and North Main lines running
west out of Edinburgh Waverley station – Edinburgh Corporation had
premises from where the city's cleansing and refuse collection operations
were conducted.

In the 1950s, when many of the citizens were being rehoused into new
council-owned accommodation from older properties, the dimensions of the
new properties were to give rise to a problem – mainly centred round pianos
of all things. Large pianos and small rooms did not sit well together and there
arose a glut of pianos – pianos which could not be negotiated through the
restricted access and doors to, and limited space within, the said properties.
Sadly, there was little or no demand for second-hand pianos at that time and
so they became a problem of disposal. Edinburgh Corporation quickly set up
a service to collect unwanted instruments and these were placed in storage in

the Russell Road premises close by the engine shed. Perhaps the Council had decided that the pianos might, at some later time, come back into favour and have a value. Whatever the reason, there was a store containing many pianos just across the railway from the shed, and herein lies my story.

It was late in the year and, during the night shift at Haymarket, whilst the supervision of cleaners was robust, there were just so many boys on duty that it was easy for a few to slip away into the dark recesses of the shed – a gloomy and dismal place even in daylight – and inevitably some new nonsense was devised. On one particular evening, using darkness as a cover in the wee small hours, a few cleaners ventured across to the Corporation's refuge disposal premises and discovered the pianos, just lying there. Not without some considerable effort on their part, a number of pianos were manhandled out of storage, up a small embankment and across four sets of running rails, almost under the noses of the signalmen in Haymarket Central Junction signal box. The raid had been well planned in advance and a depository for the purloined pianos had been well chosen. As a relic of Second World War days there were two redundant air-raid shelters – brick-built with concrete roofs, but otherwise windowless – lying empty in the shed yard. It was here that the acquired pianos were to find their way.

Now we come to the humorous aspect of the story, and humorous it indeed was. During the transfer of the pianos across the main lines, the perpetrators became aware of an approaching freight train on the Up North main line. This was a train from Thornton yard and bound for Portobello yard and was being worked 'through the town' at that ungodly hour of the morning. Putting down their burden in the 'ten foot' between the lines, they awaited the passage of the train, and one of their number, standing at the instrument, opened the lid and 'tickled the ivories', as they say. The train passed safely and the transfer across was completed.

A few days later all hell was let loose when the loss of the pianos was discovered; Lothian and Borders' finest were soon on the case. The shed and its cleaners were soon to become suspects and the police duly descended on the shed. Both the shedmaster and running foremen dismissed any suggestion that Haymarket cleaners were involved. How, it was asked, could heavy pianos be manhandled across four sets of busy running lines – for what purpose and, indeed, who would think of such a thing? Nevertheless, a full search was made, but nothing untoward was found and, in due course, apologies were made and accepted and life returned to normal, or so it seemed.

The search had missed the air-raid shelters, which were, to all intents and purposes, sealed and out of use, but it was to these shelters that attention was turned a few months later. The general-stores building was creaking at the seams and additional storage was required for some of the bulkier items, such as bales of cotton waste, firelighters and drums of cleaning material, and so the shedmaster ordered that the long-abandoned air-raid shelters be cleaned out and brought back into service as temporary-storage accommodation. This task was duly undertaken by the shed labourers and, lo and behold, there in the gloom of the shelters, the pianos were discovered. The reasons for appropriating the pianos were never to be explained and, obviously, whilst it had seemed a good idea at the time, there was no ulterior motive involved.

The discovery of the pianos then became the main talking point at the shed for several weeks and gave rise to much bothy humour. One day, in the drivers' bothy, the tale was being retold for the umpteenth time, and this time in the earshot of an elderly Thornton-based driver who was having his meal break. He listened intently and then said to the audience in the bothy, 'You dinnae ken just how pleased and relieved I am to hear what you are saying. You see, I was workin' a goods for Portobello through the toon some weeks ago and, when passing the shed and approaching Haymarket Central box, my fireman shouted to me, "Will ye come and look at this silly bugger" and, dae ye ken, there in the darkness was someone standing and playing a piano between the running lines! We thought we might report it at aither Waverley or Portobello but then, being unsure jist whit I thocht I had seen, and in discussing it with my fireman, we baith thought wha' the hell's gonny believe us, so we just kept quiet, but noo, I am really gled to ken that I wasnae really seein' things.'

This revelation set the bothy off once more!

LESS THAN GRAND OPENINGS

———◄○►———

Ceremonies for the opening of new facilities do not, as Ian Body
discovered, always goes as well as hoped

Not for the First Time

When the infant seaside resort of Weston-super-Mare got its first railway
in 1841 it was just a short Bristol and Exeter Railway branch off the main
line from Bristol towards Exeter, which was to be erratically worked for a
number of years by a team of horses and second-rate coaches. The town
commissioners at the time did not think much of this, and even less of the
fact that they were expected to pay for their own meal at the breakfast that
had been arranged to mark the opening. Local dissatisfaction also reappeared
when the Great Western Railway (GWR) was finally persuaded to put the
fast-growing town on a through loop from the main Exeter line. One local
councillor pointedly compared the GWR's hospitality shortcomings with
the lavish banquet that had been provided by the contractor who had built
the new seafront esplanade. This cloud over local railway openings was to
reappear nearly 150 years later, in September 1990.

It has always been the practice to make an event out of the opening of a
new station, irrespective of the size of the location – or lack of it. And it was
no different when Worle, on the outskirts of Weston-super-Mare, was due for
its grand unveiling. This new facility for the growing outer area of the town
had been supported by local-authority funding, and therefore the council,
not unreasonably, expected a formal event.

Unfortunately, not only did it not rate highly in railway circles, but also
most of those invited seemed to be able to find a conflicting engagement.
On top of this, it was arranged at the very last moment.

Suffice to say that the grand total of attendance was two representatives
from the council, one reporter-cum-cameraman and two staff from the West
of England's public relations office at Bristol. That might not have been too
bad had the event not solely hinged on a formal tape-cutting for the camera.
Only halfway on his journey from Bristol to Weston did the public relations

Worle station on the outskirts of Weston-super-Mare looking west towards the junction for the loop line to the town's main station in the distance..

officer (PRO) realise that the crucial element for cutting the tape – the scissors – was missing and that the options available were limited.

The local news that evening carried a very brief piece about the station, with an underwhelming piece of footage showing the local council official gamely cutting a 1ft-wide opening tape with a pair of nail scissors – which was all that the local chemist had available!

A Rather Soggy Event

Another station opening, with rather more activity, was at Pinhoe just outside Exeter on the main line to Waterloo. On 16 May 1983 local groups had rallied round and provided a healthy rent-a-crowd of schoolchildren (grateful for a day out), a brass band and even a variety of fast-food sellers sensing a quick buck.

This time, the formal part of the ceremony would be the breaking of a large banner stretched across the line, proclaiming the momentousness of the occasion; this would be done by the first train due to call. The banner was duly stretched out, whereupon a deluge occurred leaving everyone to run to the shelter of the catering tents. The first one out was the PRO, who saw that the once-proud banner was absolutely sodden, falling apart and with its lettering running badly – nothing for it but to remove it and squash it into a ball for disposal.

At this point, the divisional manager (for such was the status of the event) appeared and said to the PRO, 'Well done for protecting our banner from the rain, now let's have it out again and get the ceremony underway.' The PRO could, of course, only wonder how on earth a ball of superb papier mâché could be unrolled, ironed, repainted and displayed in the 4 minutes left before the arrival of the first train.

TRAIN 'GAPPED'

———◄◇►———

Checking delay and incident reports could be laborious, but Jim Gibbons recalls one report with a touch of humour

Reading reports by inspectors and managers could sometimes supply a lighter note to non-safety incidents. One of the hazards of the conductor rail system of electrification, apart from being close to staff walking at track level, was the loss of power to a train due to it becoming 'gapped'. Most conductor rail trains are multiple units and, therefore, have collector shoes at both ends, but a short train, particularly a two-car multiple unit, could become becalmed at a location with a long conrail gap if under the control of an unwary driver. One such driver was notorious for getting his train gapped, causing delay and disruption, whilst assistance was provided to get 'back on the juice'.

At about this time, Lord Lucan, who was wanted by the police, had disappeared and every so often a sighting would be reported somewhere in the world, followed by a media frenzy. Gapping incidents were usually investigated by a traction inspector, who would then submit a report; one such report concerning a particular recalcitrant driver on his latest escapade concluded with the sentence, 'If Lord Lucan was a gap in the conductor rail, Driver X would find him!'

THE SHOW MUST GO ON

————◄○►————

'The Radio 2 Railshow comes to town', but involved some desperate, last-minute measures on the part of Mike Lamport

In the realm of railway public relations, even after months of dedicated planning of promotional events, things could still go wrong. Or, as our former chairman Sir Peter Parker had so pithily put it, 'On the railway every day is Open Day!'

Of course, the trick was to solve the problem before anyone, the public or the media, realised it. One example of snatching success from the jaws of defeat occurred in Aberystwyth in August 1987 when the 'Radio 2 Railshow' came to town. This never-to-be-repeated tour saw the stars of BBC Radio 2 touring the UK by a specially adapted train – the BR Exhibition train – in yet another fee-earning guise. The show began in the south and west of England and then moved to Scotland, via the west coast, before calling at resorts on the east coast on its return.

With the regional public relations teams at full stretch, I, along with other members of the BRB-based PR team, were asked to help out. Our role was to liaise with local rail staff and any members of the local media who might decide to cover the story in what was, after all, the media 'silly season'. This is the time of the year when politicians – who, as we know, normally drive the news agenda – are themselves on holiday, leaving the media scrabbling around for stories.

I chose to cover the visits to Aberystwyth and Llandudno for no other reason than it gave me the opportunity to return to a holiday area favoured by the Lamport family some twenty years earlier. To reach the Cambrian coast on the evening before the show meant travelling to Shrewsbury where my Godfrey Davis 'Rail Drive' hire car awaited me at the station, and where the long, but lovely, drive westwards began.

It was a good job that I arrived in Aberystwyth when I did, as, to my horror – and to the consternation of the local staff – the train had for some reason been shunted into, and left in, what could only be described as a permanent-way depot siding! This scene of near desolation was complete with the rotting, grounded body of an old GWR coach and the usual detritus

– split-open sacks of bolts, chairs and fishplates – that one would expect to find in a working area that was normally out of the public gaze.

With the locomotive already despatched back to England for refuelling and the train now only being powered by its generator vehicle, there was no possibility of having it moved before Radio 2's presenter Ken Bruce was due 'on air' at 9.30 the next morning! This start time had been agreed so that Ken could warm up the audience, who would then be on hand to hear, and cheer, his much anticipated daily handover with Terry Wogan, who remained throughout the show in the London studio.

So while rail staff scurried around picking up the many tripping hazards and getting to work with shovels and brooms, I had to think on my feet. How was I going to hide those many immovable objects and provide a welcoming entrance to visitors drawn to the train? After all, we hoped that some of these, having been attracted by the BBC's publicity effort and having found the station, might choose to return to ride the still BR-owned Vale of Rheidol Railway.

I commandeered a telephone and eventually, just as it was closing for the day, got hold of a very helpful person in the Borough Council's Parks

At a BBC Radio 2 live show, Public Relations Officer Mike Lamport gets a hug and radio personality Gloria Hunniford a hat. (Mike Lamport)

and Gardens department. I pleaded with him for as much 'green cover' as he could muster to help hide the ramshackle buildings and to create the desperately needed welcoming feel to the station (and, of course, their town).

Sure enough, early next morning, in the style of the then popular *Challenge Anneka* programmes, a convoy of council vehicles began shuttling backwards and forwards between various parks in and around the town and the station. They even 'borrowed' large potted plants from the council offices; the scene was set just as the first visitors arrived.

With Ken broadcasting happily in the sunshine from a now tree-lined engineers' dock, I slipped away to the seafront where I was greeted by the unforgettable image of the ever-suave David Jacobs and his producer sitting side by side in deckchairs on the beach both eating ice-cream cornets. David (who, as chairman of *Juke Box Jury*, I used to watch every Saturday night as a teenager) was, as ever, dressed immaculately in blazer, shirt and tie and, if I recall correctly, was even sporting a perfectly placed pocket handkerchief.

Later that day, with disaster averted, I drove through the breathtaking Llanberis Pass, quietly reflecting that this was one of the rewards of the job but, all the while, praying that I wouldn't find myself thrown in the same situation again on my arrival in Llandudno! I needn't have worried, as Llandudno was, at that time, blessed with what seemed like acres of empty platforms and one of these had already made a good home for the train.

Next morning, everything ran like clockwork and Ken Bruce went back on air without a hitch as I handed over to my regional colleague. It was he who would see the train move next to Morecambe, where Gloria Hunniford was waiting to join the tour, along with Adrian Love, presenter of the eponymous *Love in the Afternoon* show. He would then hand over to the incomparable John Dunn who, like Terry Wogan, remained in the London studio. This then gave time each day for the train to be de-rigged and made ready to move on.

Perhaps it's no wonder that now, in my semi-retirement, I still enjoy Ken's daily show on Radio 2, often reflecting how differently things might have turned out on that sparkling summer's day nearly thirty years ago.

FALSE START

———◦►———

Geoff Body was in the wrong place at the wrong time, but at least he
got a laugh out of it

The year 1967 was quite eventful for me. As it began, I was enjoying working
as the freight sales officer for the King's Cross division. Dick Hardy was a
well-loved and respected boss and the territory included my original career
starting point, namely the Peterborough area. The passenger service on the
East Coast Main Line was our flagship activity, but the division handled some
useful freight traffic such as the Stainby iron ore, bricks from Peterborough
and even London rubbish out from Ashburton Grove to landfill sites.

In May of that year I was summoned to move back to the Liverpool
Street division to act as divisional commercial manager while the incumbent
of the post was up in York helping to plan the forthcoming merger of the
Eastern and North Eastern regions. For the next six months I got involved
in a lot of issues and projects, as everything involving business fell under my
jurisdiction. Fortunately I had been schooled in the down-to-earth activity
of the former London, Tilbury and Southend (LT&S) Line and managed
things to the apparent satisfaction of my divisional manager Harold Few.
The future seemed bright, too, as I secured an appointment to manage the
passenger promotional activity in the new combined region's headquarters
at York. But, as things turned out, that was not to be.

During this period, the Western Region was undergoing a shake-up to
replace the traditional and sometimes feudal atmosphere that had lingered
there from GWR days. I was to be part of this and replace the former
marketing and sales manager of the West of England division at Bristol, my
first senior officer appointment. The job held an immense attraction, for it
controlled a huge and complex territory, having absorbed the old Plymouth
district to create a boundary running from Worcester to Swindon to Bridport
and embracing the whole of England west thereof.

However, my first day at Bristol, just a fortnight before Christmas, was not
what I would have wanted it to be. I'd left my Enfield home very early to get
to Bristol Temple Meads at a decent time and then to walk the short distance
to the offices in Transom House where I made myself known and was ushered

into the office of Henry Sanderson, the divisional manager. Very welcoming, he also seemed surprised, and revealed that I was really supposed to be at the Paddington headquarters for a short indoctrination into the ways of the Western Region!

Unfortunately, no one had told me, so we made the best of the situation and I was invited to join in the morning conference where I met my future colleagues, including the two assistant divisional managers Clive Rowbury and Ken Painter, my opposite number on the operating side Bill Bradshaw, and various other officers, among them George Robson and Dan Reynolds representing the mechanical engineering.

All the usual subjects were covered, including the important issue of train punctuality. Unfortunately, there had been a mishap on the main line that morning when, in Robson's lurid description, a high-speed train had run into a bucket of ballast which had been overlooked during track maintenance and left in the 'four foot'. Robson reported that the collision had damaged the fairing on the front of the set, torn out various pipes along the first coaches, bruised and battered the battery boxes and generally messed up the underside of several vehicles.

In the brief silence that followed this dramatic account, Dan Reynolds added drily, 'And it didn't do the bucket much good either!'

I have remembered that moment as an amusing outcome after a poor beginning.

NORTH OF SHAFTHOLME JUNCTION

————◦►————

Donald Heath shares an amusing story passed on to him
by Tom Greaves

As recounted in the previous piece, the old Eastern and North Eastern regions were, in 1967, in the process of being amalgamated into a new super region. There was, of course, quite a long period of time between the announcement being made to the new arrangements actually being put in place, whilst people were appointed to the new posts and other organisational issues were resolved. During this period the post of chief civil engineer for the new region was announced and the holder of the same post in the old North Eastern Region was appointed to the position. His previous responsibility had commenced at the boundary between the two regions, namely Shaftholme Junction in Doncaster.

Shortly after the announcement of his new position the new appointee was at a meeting in London and decided to carry out an informal inspection of part of his extended area of responsibility by riding in the cab of the train taking him back to York. He instructed the then divisional civil engineer at King's Cross, Ken Haysom, to travel with him. They duly met on the platform on this particular day and climbed into the cab of a Deltic locomotive manned by a King's Cross crew.

The new chief civil engineer was a gentleman who possessed a distinct military style and was little given to extraneous conversation. Having made the introductions to the engine crew, not a word was said until the train rolled its way around the Offord Curves, a well-known spot just south of Huntingdon. On regaining the tangent track the new chief turned to his King's Cross subordinate and said, brusquely, 'That was not good enough, see to it, Haysom.'

Totally unprompted, the Cockney driver, overhearing this instruction, remarked, 'Core, guv, you ain't seen nothin' yet; just wait 'til you get north of Shaftholme Junction!'

A RIGHT REGULAR ROYAL TRAIN

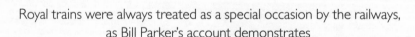

Royal trains were always treated as a special occasion by the railways, as Bill Parker's account demonstrates

After traffic apprentice (TA) training and six months as supernumerary assistant on the London, Tilbury & Southend Line (during which time I worked on the electrification, resignalling and development of the new

Ripple Lane freight railhead for two top operators, Bob Arnott and Jim Urquhart), I was formally appointed as general assistant to Cambridge District Traffic Manager Alan Suddaby. I must admit that I thought I had blown my chances of the position at the interview when, to a question from Great Eastern Line Traffic Manager Willy Thorpe about where I would live, I replied, 'I was thinking of living in Cherry Hinton,' to which he retorted, 'We don't think on the Great Eastern, we *do!*' A lesson learned!

I was placed in the operating organisation as third in line to District Operating Superintendent Harry Crosthwaite and given responsibility for passenger station and freight terminal activities, the new works section, the accident and rules and regulations section and the district operations inspectorate led by Chief District Inspector Cyril Rose. I also had a strong link with the various senior officers in the district organisation, commercial manager, motive power superintendent and finance officer – all of whom gave me very varied tasks, including investigations into the viability of, and possible improvements to, the numerous branch lines in the district.

Several weeks after my appointment, I was summoned to the divisional traffic manager's (DTM) office and, after being invited to take a seat – which in itself was a good sign – I was asked in his very military style what I knew about royal train operations. I recounted my knowledge of the special operating and signalling regulations, derived from times with my stationmaster father in Welwyn Garden City signal box as they passed by, and as a DI at King's Cross and at Peterborough when the failed engine of a Down line royal train had to be replaced in the Down main-line platform. I also mentioned being questioned there by the Duke of Edinburgh about the various procedures during the engine change and its effect on punctuality.

My boss must have had faith in me, or possibly because the customary practice was to put recent ex-TAs in at the deep end, as I was told that because Harry Crosthwaite was on leave I would take his place in charge of the royal train planning and operations for a London-bound departure three weeks hence from the royal station Wolferton on the King's Lynn–Hunstanton branch line. I was to spend a couple of days at King's Lynn and on the branch studying the layout, the signalling and station working, as well as meeting all the appropriate staff, including Wolferton Stationmaster Eddie Skillings, King's Lynn Stationmaster Billy Hill, King's Lynn Shedmaster Ted Shaw, the permanent-way inspector, signal and telegraph engineer's inspector, and the British Transport Police (BTP) inspector. A clear incentive was being authorised to stay at the famous King's Lynn Duke's Head Hotel, with authority to 'sign the bill'. Finally, as I was dismissed, feeling like a young subaltern being addressed by his CO, I heard, 'Mr Fiennes will be Officer-in-Charge of the royal train, but *you are in complete command* at King's Lynn and on the Hunstanton branch … and you will most probably be introduced to Her Majesty!'

That was the easy, short meeting! I was passed on to 'Mr Cambridge', the inimitable George Docking, who gave me a very lengthy but comprehensive briefing. I felt that he didn't have as much confidence in me, as he would be putting three DIs at King's Lynn and on the branch: Jimmy Greaves at Wolferton; Percy Baynes at King's Lynn for the engine change; and Stan Simpson in King's Lynn junction signal box, with Billy Hill on the platform. The Wolferton stationmaster would be in charge of his station and would personally receive the Queen, the Duke and other members of the royal family.

My wife was most enthusiastic to hear of my special task, and suggested that she would go to Wolferton on the big day to join the inevitable crowd. She also decided that my best suit would not be good enough, hence a visit to the famous outfitter's shop in Cambridge, Joshua Taylor!

At Wolferton station, which closed in 1969, the signal box is now a listed building. (Bill Parker)

My few days in the Lynn area were most interesting and all the staff were most informative and professional. They had done it all before, not at all blasé but determined to ensure that everything was perfect on the day. Wolferton station was particularly charming and excellently maintained. Built in 1862, the same year Queen Victoria purchased Sandringham for the Prince of Wales, it became a popular place for royal parties and international visitors travelling there by special trains. The station closed in 1969, but the buildings were purchased by a railwayman, and still stand today with a Grade II listing. The former track area is now a very smart lawn. The signal box is still in situ and is also Grade II listed.

I had done a detailed check the previous day, which I repeated after a very early breakfast on the big day itself and again an hour before the arrival of the empty royal train coaches at King's Lynn. This ensured that everyone from all departments was in place, the steam crane was 'in steam' and the standby J17 engine was on the shed in readiness. It also gave me an opportunity to check that all the level crossings were manned and that the county police would close the road and Wolferton level crossing at the predetermined time. All this was done with the assistance of a police car and driver generously allocated to me by the BT police inspector.

I kept in contact with Cambridge Deputy Chief Controller Stan Cornwell and George Docking, who was also in the control office, and with Stan Simpson in the signal box about the running of all the trains on the Cambridge line and the branch. Billy Hill and I met the empty coaches of the royal train and Officer-in-Charge Gerry Fiennes at King's Lynn and, surrounded by Ted Shaw, his mechanical foreman and Percy Baynes, oversaw the engine change on to the rear of the coaches. I then travelled with Gerry Fiennes to Wolferton.

The train was intentionally scheduled to arrive in Wolferton in very good time. The train engine was uncoupled and ran forward on to the single line towards Dersingham clear of the Up Home signal, and then ran round the train via the Up line. It then moved on to the rear of the empty coaches, coupled and propelled the coaches on to the single line again clear of the Up Home signal and then drew the empty train into the Up platform. The engine footplate stopped directly adjacent to a platelayer holding a red flag, who had been located there to ensure the doors of the saloon coach that were to be entered by the royal party were immediately alongside the red carpet. The train was now awaiting the arrival of the royal party, who were due some 25 minutes later.

Jimmy Greaves and the locomotive running foreman supervised the engine changing, with Signalman Jack Harper in the signal box working enthusiastically to their instructions. The royal luggage – which had arrived earlier and was in the royal waiting room guarded by a BT policeman – was immediately loaded on to the train by the station porter. It was supervised by the royal train manager and wagon royal train depot at Wolverton on the West Coast Main Line (WCML). The train had been prepared for an instant departure once the royal party was safely and comfortably on board. During the waiting time Gerry Fiennes took the opportunity to meet and talk to the local staff of all departments, many of whom knew him from when he was the Cambridge district operating superintendent. To me it was all a wonderful lesson in man management.

There we all were, waiting for the Queen: Eddie Skillings, smartly dressed in top hat and tails; Gerry Fiennes; the district civil engineer; the district signal and telecommunications engineer; the BT Chief Constable; Norfolk's Chief Constable; various village and county councillors; several engineering and operating department inspectors grouped nearby, 'just in case'; and me in my brand-new suit, starched white shirt, grey tie, sparkling toe caps and, of course, my bowler hat!

Behind a meagre barrier, a couple of dozen locals and visitors were held back by a pair of burly county policemen experienced, as the Norfolk Chief Constable told me, 'in crowd control'. My wife, adorned in a brand-new outfit, hat, handbag, shoes and with a dress umbrella, had no problems in getting near the front of this welcoming band of sightseers and royalists.

We had had the phone call that Her Majesty had left Sandringham. Very shortly afterwards the Rolls entered the station yard and stopped opposite the station entrance, giving me the 'tingle in my spine', which also occurred on the many future occasions when I was involved with the royal train.

Then everything seemingly happened very quickly: greetings, introductions, cheers and clapping from the crowd; Eddie Skillings accompanying the Queen, and Gerry Fiennes accompanying the Duke, on the short walk by the royal party along the red carpet to the saloon doors; and me shepherding the remaining members of the small royal party to the train where everyone was greeted by the royal train manager. Precisely at the booked departure time Gerry Fiennes gave the nod to the guard that the train could start, ourselves all joining the train, and the mechanical foreman and the district locomotive inspector travelling on the locomotive footplate.

At King's Lynn, Billy Hill met the train and Percy Baynes and the mechanical foreman oversaw the detaching of the engine and attaching of the new one, a Class J17. While this was going on the Duke strolled on to the platform and chatted with as many of us as he could in that short time. The royal train continued its journey, again on time, and I waited for my wife to arrive 20 minutes later by the local train. Then, together with Billy Hill, we went for what we all felt was a well-earned coffee!

Back in the district office I was summoned by Alan Suddaby and advised, with a smile, that Mr Fiennes was very pleased and felt that everything had gone perfectly. In order to expand my experience, Fiennes had decided that any future royal trains to and from Wolferton and elsewhere in the district would be my job. Also, if the train officer-in-charge agreed, I could travel on the train all the way to London!

The whole event from planning to completion had been an exceptional initiation and an uplifting experience for me. I felt privileged to have been given the opportunity to serve the royal family and to work with experienced, highly competent and enthusiastic railwaymen, especially one of the best railway operators of all times – Gerry Fiennes. However, it was kept in perspective by the comment from my wife, remarking, 'I'm glad you didn't mess about with those dirty oily couplings and the coal and soot on the footplate – and there's not even a speck of dust on your new suit!'

REWARD?

————◄○►————

Geoff Body was sent on an unexpected and unusual trip from
London to Scotland

Summer 1961 was drawing to a close as I was summoned from my desk to the line-traffic manager's office in Saracen's Head House near Fenchurch Street station. What, I wondered, was this all about?

The development of passenger-party travel was one of my varied responsibilities as head of the sales and development section for the LT&S Line and it was explained to me that, at this time of year, the Caledonian

Steam Packet Company provided a short visit to their steamers operating in the Firth of Clyde for selected staff who might influence business.

I had been chosen to go as a reward for my hard work, explained John W. Dedman. Commercial Manager Ted Taylor later put it differently: 'You were the one we could most spare,' he said with a familiar half grin.

Anyway, off I duly set on the journey to Glasgow Central, registering at the hotel and settling into a rather nice room there. There was a pre-dinner gathering, with drinks for the group of select people to get to know each other and their hosts. A fine meal followed and then my introduction to malt whisky – all a rather unaccustomed measure of high living for me.

Our first full day started with a good breakfast and a train journey along the north bank of the River Clyde to get to Balloch at the southern end of Loch Lomond. There we joined the elegant paddle steamer *Maid of the Loch*, which was later to grace the front cover of my first hardback book. Coffee and pastries were supplied as we steamed the length of the loch to Ardlui where lunch had been arranged. Replete and not a little sleepy we cruised back south again, returned to Glasgow for another journey, via Wemyss Bay, and then took a steamer to Rothesay for our dinner and night's stay there. It had been a good day and I could see myself recommending this sort of thing without reservation.

In September 1961 the turbine steamer *Duchess of Hamilton* heads along the Firth of Clyde near Largs.

With her paddles creating a strong wake, PS *Caledonia* sets off from Rothesay for her next stop at Dunoon.

Breakfast the following morning was lavish, but no sooner were we on the steamer than another one was served, to be followed by coffee and snacks and an early arrival at Millport on Great Cumbrae Island where, it turned out, we were to have lunch! By the time we had cruised back – with afternoon tea! – along the Kyles of Bute and then to Dunoon where we had dinner in another nice hotel, I had severe doubts about the ability of my trouser waistband to last the remainder of my time here. They were temporarily relieved by the pressing invitation to join in an evening of lively Scottish music and even livelier dancing.

Dragged unwillingly from sleep, the next day was to prove another experience marathon. Our vessel steamed its way over to Arran for a landing at Brodick Pier, lunch in a nearby hotel and then a trip in a nice little Bedford Duple Vista coach to a charming pub near Bennan Head on the southern extremity of the road that runs right round the island. It was a lovely, restful place, but the second midday meal was definitely not needed. Politeness demanded a token gesture, and the same on the eventual water crossing back to the mainland at Ardrossan.

I managed to function fairly normally on the train back to Glasgow, but a grand, final dinner proved my match and after contributing to the warm thanks to our hosts I slipped thankfully away to the quiet of my room. All too generous and lavish perhaps, but it had been a wonderful experience for me, and a useful one, too. I had warmed to the quiet majesty of the scenery and to the genuine people of the area, and I had noted the admirable efficiency with which the whole tourist activity was served – all features I could genuinely pass on. Albeit nearing great change, this was still part of the great Clyde steamer era when one could marvel a little longer at the skills of vessel crews and harbour staff in their judgements and manoeuvres of dozens of vessels and see the immaculate vessels themselves and their gleaming, pulsating engine rooms as something rather special.

The whole tour had been so efficiently arranged, and I had been greatly impressed by the train and steamer service pattern that constituted the transport arteries of the area. Shunting at Ripple Lane and ship to wagon unloading at Poplar Dock were going to be stark contrasts when I got back, and our little ferry out of Tilbury would seem a rather puny affair after the wonders of the Clyde.

THE BR REPRESENTATIVE – FOR RABBITS!

The fairy-tale image of rabbits was not shared by working railwaymen – and certainly not on one occasion by Jim Dorward

It is Wednesday 1 June 1960 and I am on the 4.39 p.m. from Forfar to Perth which, as the 3.30 p.m. from Aberdeen to Glasgow (Buchanan Street), carries the Aberdeen portion of the time-critical West Coast Travelling Post Office as far as Perth. I am on my way back from Perth from, of all things, the annual general meeting (AGM) of a rabbit clearance society.

As rabbits were widespread and causing much damage in the countryside, the Perth district engineer decided that BR should join the various rabbit clearance societies that were being formed to fight the problem. The cost of each member's subscription was based on the acreage of land owned, with the money that was collected paying the wages of rabbit trappers. So, as the most junior person in the drawing office − 17 years of age − I was given the task of working out the acreage of railway land covered by each society and then arranging BR's membership. Understandably, this resulted in invitations being sent to BR to attend the AGMs of the various societies. As circumstances conspired, I became the 'BR representative' and was told to attend these AGMs, mainly as a matter of BR courtesy.

This had not been a problem, until now, as I only had to write a short report on the outcomes for my immediate boss. However, at the AGM in Forfar, the chairman welcomed BR as a member and then promptly asked the 'BR representative' to explain to the large gathering of farmers, the connection between rabbits and trains!

Needless to say I was flabbergasted. I was concerned that what was to be my first attempt at public speaking was going to get back to the district engineer, who was sponsoring my civil-engineering studentship. Simultaneously, I was desperately trying to recall what I had been told back in the office about track subsidence, thinking that there must be some similarity between coal-mining subsidence and damage caused by tunnelling rabbits.

As I stood up, heads turned to see who was going to give the requested explanation. Trying to appear authoritative and sound as though I knew all about permanent-way maintenance, if not rabbits, I blurted out a few remarks about the possibility of 15mph speed restrictions, as in the Fife coalfield. On reflection, this must have seemed ludicrous to the farmers, especially as they must see the Glasgow−Aberdeen trains charging along at 80mph on the Perth district's best track! I was now very worried about the possibility of being called into the district engineer's office or of seeing 'Rabbits Slash Train Speeds' headlined in the local newspaper!

With hindsight, what I should have said is that rabbits, despite having a cute reputation as Peter Rabbit or Bugs Bunny, are capable of causing considerable damage. When they burrow into man-made embankments formed of earth, for instance, they create a series of tunnels. Heavy pounding by passing trains squashes these, resulting in uneven track subsidence and track geometry defects that can cause derailments if they are not quickly rectified.

Three years after my performance at the Forfar AGM, and perhaps with the help of the rabbit-clearance societies, 80mph trains running in the area was very much a part of the great A4 Pacific locomotive swansong when, displaced by the introduction of Deltic diesels on the East Coast Main Line, engines such as 4-6-2 No. 60019 *Bittern* were transferred to the Scottish Region to work the new 3-hour Glasgow–Aberdeen via Forfar expresses.

KNOWING ONE'S PLACE

———◁○▷———

Things were done in a certain, prescribed way at Worcester, as
Ian Body soon found out

Arriving for my first 'real' job as assistant area manager at Worcester, I was impressed during the first few weeks to be in receipt of a goodly number of gifts – nets of sprouts, sacks of potatoes, bags of apples and blackberries – either left in my office at Worcester Shrub Hill or sitting with my name on at places along the Cotswold Line during my station visits. Of course, I enquired as to whom they were from or what they were for but received no enlightenment.

One night fairly soon after my arrival I was called out to a freight derailment in the small yard at Evesham. It was early on in my operating experience and this was my first derailment, so I decided to play safe. On arrival at Evesham signal box at the entrance to the yard, I duly signed the train register and then sensibly, I thought, asked the signalman for his advice on what should be done.

What followed did not clarify the immediate issue, but it did solve the riddle of the fruit and vegetable largesse. The signalman's response was simply, 'I work the box, sir, and you take all the decisions. That's why you get the fruit and veg as compensation!'

POLMONT 1984

————◦————

Peter Whittaker had a tense moment with the Railway Inspectorate
after the Polmont derailment

As acting director of operations at the BRB, I arrived home after a particularly difficult Monday to hear the first reports of a serious railway accident near Falkirk in Scotland. With a sinking feeling I realised that this would be my first contact with the Railway Inspectorate as the official voice of BR.

I clearly needed to acquaint myself with as many facts as possible and so arrived early in the office the next morning to find that my good friend Chris Green (at that time deputy general manager of the Scottish Region) had arrived before me after travelling from Glasgow on the sleeper. He was able to give me a very full briefing before the inevitable call came from Freddie Rose, then Chief Inspecting Officer.

To refresh memories, the Polmont accident the previous evening had resulted in thirteen fatalities and sixty-one injured passengers, some serious, when an Edinburgh–Glasgow train had been derailed following a collision at 85mph with a stray cow on the line. This was a push–pull unit with the locomotive at the rear and I was aware that concerns had been expressed about the effect on emergency braking and derailment of this formation.

Once I had given Freddie Rose all the details that I knew at that stage, there came one of those career-defining (or threatening) moments. 'I assume you will be taking these units out of service today,' said the Chief Inspecting Officer. Visions arose of the chaos that would result from any such decision! Swallowing very hard, I replied, 'Come off it Freddie, for one freak accident, you must be joking!' I waited for the explosion at the other end of the line but after what seemed an eternity he said something like, 'I suppose you're right.'

There followed an anxious wait for the official accident report some months later. The accident did generate considerable, sometimes acrimonious, debate about the safety of push–pull trains on BR, and myself and others wondered what criticism or recommendations might be contained in the report. In the event, Inspecting Officer Tony King confined his recommendations to the fitting of object deflectors and headlights, and improvements to fencing.

JOINT ROAD AND RAIL OFFICE

An unusual period in Geoff Body's career, something of a tributary, at least improved the household budget

After a post-National Service stint on early and late turns in the booking office at Biggleswade I was ready for a change. We had managed to set up our first home in a pleasant rented house along the Great North Road towards Sandy, but on just over £5 a week could only manage the barest of furnishing and living standards. Sunday pay was a godsend and even the small commission from selling Railway Passengers Assurance helped.

Then came a vacancy list advertising a Class IV post in the joint road and rail office, located at Finsbury Park. I could get there by train and resolved to have a go. Surprised, I had a good interview, was appointed and duly arrived on the starting date to find that the offices were on two floors above the Silver Bullet pub. That, at least, was handy.

We were just a small unit of four people, beside myself: Tom Gregory, the Special Class B boss, who was rarely in; Class II Jimmy Justice; Class V John Moody; and our secretary and typist Christine Sharpe.

Jimmy was the brains, John kept the records and my job, apparently, was to prepare briefs for our solicitors. Under the 1933 Road and Rail Traffic Act, road hauliers seeking new or additional vehicle licences had to apply to, in our case, the chairman of the Metropolitan Traffic Commissioners, and he would publicise their applications, receive objections from legitimate existing transport providers and hold a judicial hearing where appropriate.

The published 'Applications and Decisions' covered everything from a 'C' licence for carrying one's own goods to a 'B' licence for carrying specific goods for other people, and then an 'A' licence allowing the operator to carry anything anywhere. Among the latter were ambitions that could seriously erode existing rail business and we had every right to enter an objection and instruct counsel to oppose the application for us. In the really important cases this might be a QC, one or two of whom put up some very lively performances in the stylised traffic court procedures of opening and closing statements, presentation of witnesses and evidence, cross-examination and so on.

My contribution was to prepare a brief with what we knew about the applicant's activities and the facilities we had for handling whatever goods movement the applicant was seeking. Jim was the usual back-up in court but I got to go fairly often and did my job of drawing our counsels' attention to relevant information. On one or two occasions I found myself doing the front-line job because our advocate was late or missing, but fortunately I survived the ordeal.

This was not a job that made me a better railwayman, but it was interesting. On my train journeys I prepared for my various Institute of Transport examinations – on some winter journeys with ice on the inside of the carriage windows. With Jim and John I frequented Highbury and White Hart Lane in the days when no one sat at a football match and crush barriers were a godsend. I used trams to get to the traffic courts and spent lunch times either in the Silver Bullet, around the local antique shops or rowing on Finsbury Park Lake. The time was coming to move out of this specialised environment but, among the privilege of witnessing some very exciting legal battles, I most vividly remember something rather less grand.

In court, waiting for the case to which we had objected, the clerk called forward an applicant who held an 'F' licence for carrying his own produce as a farmer. He could already take his sugar beet to the BSC factory at Felstead and, quite reasonably, sought to be allowed to do the same for other local growers. There was no opposition and the chairman needed only to word the new licence in terms of the radius to which it should be limited. The farmer seemed bemused by being asked for the mileage to Felstead, so the chairman rephrased his request as, 'How far is it as the crow flies?'

'I don't know, your honour, I've never done it that way.' His flippant reply rather made the day for the whole court.

ANGLIA REGION CONTROL OFFICE

————◀◦▶————

*Friends had told Chris Blackman that Liverpool Street was a good place
to work – he was not to be disappointed*

As the new year of 1988 opened I took up the post of operations planning manager for the new Anglia Region. Overseeing the day-to-day train performance for the region was the responsibility of the Regional Control, each shift being run by a deputy chief controller (DCC). It was a curious title, as the person he reported in to was never titled or even referred to as the chief controller; instead, it was operating (or operations) officer.

As well as being responsible for co-ordinating the immediate response to train failures, mishaps and other eventualities affecting train running, the DCC would maintain a log of such events and the actions taken. One of the DCCs, Bob Mace, took particular pride in the quality and style of the reporting in his log. Thus, a report of cattle on the line would be headed 'Bovine Incursion'; similarly, sheep on the line was 'Ovine Incursion', and horses 'Equine Incursion'.

One morning, services were interrupted by the presence of a goat on the line at Bishopsgate just outside Liverpool Street. How it got there we never discovered, but Bob duly sorted the problems it caused and trains were soon running normally again whilst Bob made his entry into the log and prepared to give it a title. But what was the appropriate adjective for goat? For once he was stumped – just momentarily, for he then remembered that Richard Morris the Anglia Region operations manager had a degree in Classics, so he would be bound to know.

Bob stood up, strode out of the office, turned right down the corridor then left into Richard's office.

'Morning guv, what's the adjective associated with goat?'

'Caprine!' was the immediate response. Bob did an about-turn, hastened back down the corridor to the control office and completed the entry with the title 'Caprine Incursion'.

Two weeks later Bob was on late turn when there was an interruption to the region's services, which Bob duly logged as caused by 'a llama and its friend an emu on the railway line', but when it came to finishing the entry with a title Bob was once again stumped. Without further hesitation he shot out of the office, down the corridor and into 'the Governor's office'. However, with remarkable foresight, Richard Morris had chosen not to be in the office that afternoon so was not available for his reputation to be sorely tested.

Bob returned slowly to his own office, pondered a moment and then with a flourish entitled the entry 'Zoological Incursion'!

Out at the site of this zoological incursion the local, permanent-way gang had rounded up the llama and returned it to its owner, but the emu was last seen running away towards London on the Up line. The signalman, with commendable presence of mind and devotion to duty, proceeded to carry out Absolute Block Regulation 23 and sent the bell signal 4-5-5 for, in this case, 'an emu running away in right direction'!

HONESTLY, I WANT TO PAY FOR A TRAIN

————◄○►————

In a literal sense Ian Body's bit of Long Marston local enterprise only paid off in goodwill

Back in the 1970s all railway activity was managed by a host of clerks and recorders who were just as able to prevent things happening as to be able to facilitate them.

Out at Long Marston was Bird's scrap-metal facility and one day when the local manager was paying a visit the owners asked if an additional service could be provided at short notice. The manager duly approached the divisional office, which managed to find sufficient reasons to refuse the request. Undaunted, the manager decided it could be done locally and so identified a rake of empties which were then suitably loaded. At the time there was a locomotive on a long layover whose driver was willing to make an additional run rather than sit around bored. Suffice to say that this 'ghost train' was able to run to Burnt Oak, near Birmingham, as a special and then offload and return to Long Marston. The Total Operations Processing System (TOPS) recorded the wagons as not having moved and no one apparently noticed the additional fuel used by the locomotive.

More impressive than this piece of instant business was the fact that for two weeks the divisional freight office stubbornly denied all attempts to confirm the train's existence and bill the willing customer. So in the end everyone just gave up trying. Sad, but a great boost for our link with the substantial Long Marston activity and an equal boost for the local manager when it came to Christmas.

HAPPY BIRTHDAY

—◇—

Don Love's 48th birthday was memorable for a locomotive naming ceremony by Dame Elisabeth Schwarzkopf

In 1984 I was in my fifth year as area manager at Liverpool Street station, London. Out of the blue I was asked to officiate at a locomotive-naming ceremony at my station on the 8 June, which happened to be my 48th birthday. I was informed that a Class 47 diesel locomotive was to be named *Aldeburgh Festival* by Dame Elisabeth Schwarzkopf, who was connected with the festival. As an opera fan myself, I knew she was a world-famous operatic soprano and I looked forward to this opportunity to meet her.

The project was initiated by Sir Richard Cave, then a member of the BRB and also chairman of Thorne EMI, owner of the HMV record label, amongst others. Schwarzkopf's late husband was Walter Legge, the classical record producer for EMI in post-war years. The project involved the naming ceremony in the morning and a special train for the Aldeburgh Festival opera-goers in the afternoon.

This was to be a trial run to emulate Glyndebourne's railway connection and I was well aware of the Glyndebourne arrangements from my days as operating officer on the Brighton line in the 1970s when I enjoyed the benefit of complimentary tickets for rehearsals.

Come the day for our event, everything was organised. Schwarzkopf would arrive by air from Switzerland in the morning and a room was booked in the Great Eastern Hotel next to the station for her to change in.

The plan was to hold a briefing in the banqueting room and then walk to platform 9 where the highly polished locomotive would be positioned and fitted with a small curtain over the new nameplate.

A small rostrum was erected adjacent to the nameplate, with a public address microphone for the unveiling, speech and photographs, all to be followed by a champagne reception in the banqueting hall. In the afternoon the special train for Aldeburgh would be hauled by the newly named locomotive, with three guests and myself on board in addition to the regular opera-goers on their way to attend the evening performance of Benjamin Britten's *Albert Herring*.

We waited in the banqueting room for the diva to make her entrance. Her stepdaughter explained to me that her full title was Doctor (not Dame) Elisabeth Legge-Schwarzkopf. She entered right on time and I was able to brief her, although her command of English was not complete as her native language was German. I recalled that Walter Legge had arranged for her debut at Covent Garden, which did not suit her because operas there were then all performed in English. Our briefing became an occasion for replacing some words with those more easily understood and pronounced.

All set, I put on my bowler hat and we proceeded with Sir Richard in elegant fashion across the old footbridge, only to stop at the top of the steps down to platform 9. Doctor Schwarzkopf had seen some of my cleaners busily sweeping the steps and exclaimed, 'The dust! My throat!' I promptly diverted my sweepers and we duly arrived at the rostrum beside the locomotive to a small crowd consisting of fans and passengers who applauded the diva's arrival.

I made an introduction and speeches were given; the little curtain was opened, revealing the brass nameplate, and the locomotive was named. I was later told that the microphone was not working because a tractor with a trolley full of mailbags had crossed and cut the cable – nobody noticed! Autographs were then signed and I assembled the party, with a few extra fans, to return across the footbridge to the hotel.

On the way we were accosted by a man I recognised as Edward Greenfield, the music critic of the *Guardian* newspaper, who had recently purchased a town house in nearby Spitalfields. He and Schwarzkopf knew each other and he invited her to his house. To avoid the attempted hijack I explained the situation to him and invited him to accompany us to the reception.

Aided by champagne, the reception went well. Schwarzkopf asked me about the bowler hat I wore and we rehearsed the pronunciation! She was about 69 then and had retired from public performance, holding master classes instead. In her conversation with Edward Greenfield she did express critical views on some of the younger singers of the day.

Of course, I obtained her autograph and one of the fans asked to see it; it was large and formed in the shape of a heart. I was told that I was much favoured! With the performance over, the diva returned to her room and then began her journey back to Switzerland.

It was during the reception that my operations assistant discreetly informed me of the bad news that we had no guard for the train. The good news for me was that there hadn't been many advance bookings so we were able to accommodate them all in one carriage. An extra, very clean carriage was added to the rear of the then regular afternoon Lowestoft train, which was to be hauled by the newly named *Aldeburgh Festival* locomotive. Champagne was served en route. All would be well – and was!

The poor bookings meant that the special train was not tried again. However, Elisabeth Schwarzkopf was created a Dame of the British Empire eight years later.

NO. 1 PUMP HOUSE, SUDBROOK

Geoff Body retains vivid memories of this building and the role it played in keeping the Severn Tunnel dry

During my time as marketing and sales manager for the West of England Division, based at Bristol, I had the opportunity to visit the Severn Tunnel main pumping station at Sudbrook on the west bank of the Severn. After fourteen years of every conceivable kind of difficulty, the 4-mile, 628yd bore under the River Severn had been opened in 1886. Twice during the tunnel's construction it was flooded when the 'Great Spring' broke in and an abnormal tidal wave drowned the workings on yet another occasion.

Now well harnessed, the Great Spring still has to be managed and land water also drains into the tunnel from the surrounding land mass. There are five pumping shafts to contain this flow, which amounts to around 20 million gallons on an average day, but has risen as high as 29.5 million, and once much higher still.

Originally the tunnel was kept dry by six 70in Cornish beam engines, with four smaller beam engines at two of the subsidiary shafts. I was never to see these monsters, nor the long bank of boilers which fed them, at work but they were still in position at the time of my visit. Far more impressive – and costly to operate – than the bank of electric impeller pumps which replaced them, the beam engines' sheer size was magnificent, a feature that their modern replacements did not possess.

The changeover from the traditional steam power for the massive beam engines and the huge fans which kept the tunnel ventilated, to the 3.300V

The beams of the massive Cornish pumping engines in the Severn Tunnel's No. 1 Pump House at Sudbrook.

This row of boilers supplied steam for the Severn Tunnel pumping engines prior to their replacement by electric pumps.

electricity supply for impeller pumps and their attendant sensor equipment also gave the main pump house a new, modern control room where manager Bruce Pearce presided and acted as my tour guide. The whole function within this ugly, square No. 1 Pump House was impressive, but more sensations were to come via a quite ordinary door in a lower room that led directly to a walkway running down a long, narrow passage. Through the apertures in the latticed metal underfoot rushed the waters of the Great Spring, contained but intense, urgent and never ceasing or hesitating.

The end of the walkway led to another unassuming door. It opened on to the tunnel itself and the sheer presence of the bore was astonishing, which was heightened as passenger trains sped smoothly past or a long coal train out of Severn Tunnel Junction yard eased slightly after the descent from the Welsh end became the 1 in 100 climb out again.

I had learned much of this major piece of civil engineering, including something about the task of its maintenance, from inside and above. I had also stood inside the bore and been able to get some understanding of what it might have been like when completely flooded back in 1880 and Diver

Lambert had struggled through the sodden construction debris with untried breathing apparatus to turn off a critical valve.

THE RAILWAY INSPECTORATE

———◄○►———

Bill Parker's involvement with the Railway Inspectorate included key tunnel and level crossing events

The Ministry of Transport Railway Inspectorate (HMRI) comprised senior Royal Engineers (RE) officers, all very competent in railway operations and engineering and who had been involved with the military railway depot at Longmoor. Formed in 1840 by the Board of Trade to investigate railway accidents and to approve new and important changes to the railways, its first accident inquiry was the train crash at Howden in that same year. Investigations were held in public and the detailed and uncompromising reports included the reasons for the accident and recommendations to avoid recurrences; the latter were accepted and applied by the railway companies.

The Inspectorate ceased in 1990, its role taken over by the Health and Safety Executive (which itself was taken over by the Office of Rail Regulation), with the last RE officer retiring in 1988. For over thirty years I had the privilege and great pleasure of being associated with most of the officers of the Inspectorate, my first when I attended HMRI and BR meetings as a newly appointed junior member in the Eastern Region's headquarters rules and regulations section in the early 1950s. The Divisional Assistant Operating Superintendents Gerry Fiennes and Jim Royston had decreed that new staff should attend formal meetings with the Inspectorate regarding operational matters, but just to listen and learn – not to speak unless invited to do so!

I was to be the first member of staff under this arrangement. There was I, a young railwayman in my early 20s and a former lowly relief stationmaster and National Service NCO, surrounded by very senior engineers – a brigadier and a colonel, no less. They, much more than some of my railway colleagues, generously encouraged me to feel a member of the railway team,

Brigadier Langley commenting humorously that they should watch their ways, as they had with them 'a very young railwayman from the sharp-end'. And, looking at me, he added, 'Over lunch you can tell me about all the rules you have broken up to now.' Not likely, I thought, but how did he know!

As London Euston divisional operating superintendent, I was next involved (along with IOs Colonel Robertson, Lieutenant Colonel McNaughton and Colonel Reed) in the 1960s inspection of the WCML electrified railway between Rugby and Euston and the power signal boxes at Euston, Willesden, Watford, Bletchley and Rugby. The former inspections were undertaken in the divisional saloon, propelled by a diesel locomotive.

The inspections in the tunnels in the division intrigued me, particularly Kilsby (about 5 miles south of Rugby) and those approaching Euston. I had walked them all, accompanied by Divisional Civil Engineer Leslie Sloane, whose explanation of Kilsby's history I especially recall. It was the longest tunnel in the network and was more expensive than forecast. It also took much longer to build than expected because of unexpected quicksands, which were not revealed in the trial borings, causing the tunnel roof to collapse and flood the tunnel. Sloane had stressed that it was a 'very wet tunnel' and insisted on our wearing extensive wet-weather clothing – from steel hat and waterproofs down to wellies. I still got very wet and dirty from the considerable and continuous falling muddy water but we were able to have early access to a relatively nearby hotel for a pint or two and a bath.

This was almost a 'full-frontal' in tunnel-roof terms, especially when I ventured outside with IOs Colonel Robertson and Colonel Reed and was sprayed again by lots of dirty, muddy water; I was invited to scoop some of the mud off the tunnel roof to appreciate the very real maintenance problems. I became very sympathetic for the local permanent way and electrical overhead equipment staff. The air vents were included in our tour and I saw the upper structures later from the M45 looking like Martello towers and quite out of keeping in a field of animals!

The inspections of the power signal boxes were fascinating, as was a totally different association with Colonel Reed involving the 'in-public inspection' of the auto-barrier crossing near Lidlington on the Bedford–Bletchley line, which required approval by him. This installation was one of the first of its kind on the network and such a completely new-style level crossing – unmanned and without gates – was an extremely sensitive change and understandably engendered serious local concern. We expected a 'rough ride' at the meeting of some sixty or so members of the public, comprising local

The ventilation shafts for Kilsby Tunnel are topped by round castellated towers. (Bill Parker)

village people, school teachers, councillors and their senior staff from local authorities and a strong media presence. Everyone was either opposed to the change or very wary of it.

After introductions and my brief explanation, demonstrations followed of the operation of the flashing lights and warning bells – and the flashing 'second train coming' – all of which were given practical expression by means of specially arranged train movements simulating real, live situations. These operations were supported by frequent verbal explanations by my technical colleagues and myself.

These demonstrations lasted for almost 90 minutes and many questions inevitably followed. Some were hard-hitting, alleging the indifferent attitude of the railway management and the government's Ministry of Transport

(MoT) to the safety of the public – children, the elderly and handicapped, vehicles and their drivers and passengers etc. Moreover, despite the accuracy, honesty, firmness and sensitivity of our answers, some scepticism and the occasional vitriolic comment still continued from a few of the more argumentative members of the public. On the whole, the questions were relevant and well balanced, but people were genuinely frightened of this new-fangled piece of unmanned equipment.

Throughout the meeting, Colonel Reed held it together in a firm but most charming way and invited me to go through all the publicity efforts we had made to explain the changes and reassure everyone affected. It became clear to him that the consultation had reached its finality and, in a most diplomatic, sensitive and understanding manner, he obtained confirmation from those present that they had received and understood everything BR had done and the vital importance of always responding to the lights and bells. On that note, he concluded by saying he was satisfied with the comprehensive and detailed actions BR had undertaken and that he formally approved the introduction of the auto-barrier crossing. He also confirmed that I had arranged for a crossing keeper to remain at the crossing in an advisory capacity for six months.

After over 100 years of manned gates which encompassed the whole width of the roadway, this new installation involved a complete change in level-crossing operation. Thankfully my regular reports of the operation of the barriers etc. by the temporary crossing keepers and regular visits by my DIs and senior managers, including myself, indicated successful and safe operations by the public and all road users.

RAILWAY INSPECTORATE INQUIRIES

————◦►————

Bill Parker was also involved with the Railway Inspectorate in the course of three specific accident investigations

Fortunately I had to manage only three accidents at which a public MoT inquiry had to be held. The first two associations were with Colonel Reed in the 1960s when I was London Euston divisional operating superintendent.

During the modernisation of the southern end of the WCML, a contractor's crane working on the Up lines near Hemel Hempstead and, holding a length of track in a suspended position, fell forward and hit the side and roof of two coaches of an Up main-line express passenger train, which was fortunately passing very slowly on the Down main line during single-line working (SLW). Two coaches were derailed and about fifty passengers were injured, fortunately not seriously. The cause was established as a metal fracture on the crane.

My other involvement with Colonel Reed was on the Midland Main Line when a bogie wheel on a passenger carriage of an Up main-line express passenger train fractured as it passed over a series of points at West Hampstead and caused several coaches to be derailed. The train was slowing down approaching St Pancras, and although the track and coach damage was extensive, fortunately there were few passenger casualties, with only one young lady being retained in hospital. As it was a few days before Christmas, I had the pleasant duty of taking her flowers and chocolates. The cause of this accident was clearly a metal fault in the bogie wheel.

The third accident for which a public MoT inquiry was held was several years later when I was Birmingham assistant divisional manager and acting divisional operating superintendent. The Up line 2.15 p.m. four-car electric multiple unit (EMU) from Wolverhampton High Level station ran headlong into a diesel locomotive hauling a Down line freight train of thirty-two loaded steel wagons from Chesterfield. The freight train was moving slowly on the Down line under clear signals and was about to cross from the Down line, over the Up line and into an Up-side steel railhead at Monmore Green, Wolverhampton.

The EMU, travelling at 45mph, collided head-on with the front of the diesel locomotive and rose upwards into the 25KV overhead-line equipment. There was extensive damage to the locomotive and its 500-gallon fuel tank, resulting in a severe fire. Several of the steel wagons were also damaged. Very sadly, both drivers were killed and thirty-two passengers were injured, but no one was detained in hospital. The second man, on seeing the approaching EMU, was able to jump from the cab and suffered only minor injuries.

At that time there was a track circuit failure which caused the first colour light signal to be held at red after leaving Wolverhampton High Level station. As no indication could be given of when the track circuit failure would be resolved, the EMU experienced a delayed start of 7 minutes. The signalman in Wolverhampton power signal box shouted to the driver to pass the red signal at danger and proceed at caution. This instruction was confirmed by the signal-box regulator inspector and the station foreman; nonetheless, the train seemed to accelerate rapidly.

The EMU driver, as authorised, passed the affected signal at red, and also passed the next colour light signal, which was protecting the movement of the steel train on the Down line and its crossing of the Up line into the steel railhead. The EMU then ran through trailing points and over the crossover on to the Down line and collided head-on at 45mph with the locomotive of the steel train. The basic cause of this accident was clearly a signal irregularly passed at danger.

The public inquiry was conducted by Major Olver and Lieutenant Colonel Ian McNaughton. It was Olver's first inquiry of his appointment; he had spent a month with me in the Euston division as part of his final training. The inquiry was held in a large, local church hall and was attended by more than fifty people, many of whom were railwaymen of all grades and departments, trade union representatives and relatives and friends of the casualties. Many of them accepted the IO's invitation to ask questions, all in a very constructive and calmly dignified manner. The local media was also represented.

The divisional operating assistant at the time was the excellent operator Peter Rayner, who was especially supportive. He had taken charge of the accident site and undertaken extensive research with the engineers there, as well as at Wolverhampton power signal box and with all the staff of the various departments involved.

The cause, as concluded by my local departmental inquiry and confirmed by the IOs, was that the second of the red colour light signals had been passed at danger irregularly and that the EMU driver was responsible for this major accident. But why would an experienced driver do this? The reason could only be a matter for conjecture. Perhaps he was just anxious to recover lost time. Perhaps he might have misread the colour light signals ahead, as there was one some 700yd beyond the one he passed that was irregularly showing green. The IO recommended a change to the signalling interlocking to ensure that in such circumstances the signal should show a red aspect.

The IOs always had the benefit of the report of its departmental inquiry produced by BR, and these were always held very shortly after an accident and received by the HMRI before their own inquiries. The divisional operating superintendent or his assistant chaired these inquiries, supported by the divisional civil engineer, mechanical and electrical engineer and signal and telecommunications engineer. Their reports were extremely detailed and comprehensive, covering the evidence of the witnesses, its analysis and conclusions as to the cause of the accident and who was responsible for it.

My future association with the Inspectorate was somewhat limited – informally when I was at BR headquarters and also when I was divisional manger at King's Cross regarding the plans for the electrification from Royston–Cambridge and Hitchin–Huntingdon. I also had the pleasure of some unofficial discussions with IO Major Peter Olver who, when I retired from BR, offered me the opportunity of joining the Inspectorate, which I had to decline because of other formal work commitments.

Working with the Inspectorate and its highly competent staff was for me, and I am certain to all my operating and engineering colleagues, a very fruitful, valuable and enjoyable experience.

LODGINGS AND DIGS

———◄○►———

Many railwaymen in relief or similar jobs, Geoff Body among them,
had to find accommodation away from home

Prior to moving to London when appointed as head of the cartage and terminals sub-section in the office of the London (suburban) district goods manager I had to find lodgings while the house hunting went on. How I came to lodge with a couple in Palmers Green I cannot now recall, but they were nice folk – she outgoing and motherly and he a bit severe (he became the head of a print chapel, a somewhat contentious business in those days). Each day I caught a train from Palmers Green to Gordon Hill and carried out a small ritual en route.

My landlady had, I thought, asked if I liked bread and butter pudding, which I did. But she was in fact asking about my regard for bread pudding, for which I had none. Thus it came about that instead of a favourite pudding with my evening meal I was handed a large, wrapped lump of bread pudding as I left the house each morning. Safely on board my regular train, down would come the carriage window and out would go the bread pudding. What the local lengthman made of this phenomenon I shall never know, but my landlady would have been heartbroken had I spurned her goodwill – or known what I was doing with it! Lesser of two evils.

On beginning my TA training I again needed lodgings and our local Methodist minister kindly offered to arrange something with his opposite number in Spalding, my first posting. The latter had clearly twisted the arm of a couple of maiden ladies who obviously did not relish my presence and, I suspected, bolted their doors and crossed themselves before retiring in the same house as this unwelcome visitor. Fortunately I got on well with the Spalding goods agent – an able, likeable man of classical tastes – and I was invited to move my lodgings to his home.

Next I was off to Whitemoor yard, which fixed me up nicely with the Brands – she a kindly soul, he a dedicated and skilled top link driver. They even provided me with a bicycle – essential for getting around the area, especially when on shifts. My hosts were used to us two men coming and going at almost any time – he to take up his rostered loco diagram and me to start an early, late or night turn.

The last lodge came with the advent of my Cambridge training period when, and again I cannot remember how, I finished up in the garret of an elderly couple, who were both pleasant but somewhat Dickensian in demeanour and lifestyle. Their pleasure and practice was to feed me promptly after I got in and then take what change they could from me in games of rummy in which they spared no quarter.

After training, I was posted as assistant stationmaster at Clacton and I was able to have my family in 'digs' with me for the summer season, marking the end of the 'lodging' years. Thousands of railwaymen had similar experiences while many others stayed nights in hostels as part of an overnight turn. Such places were rarely built for any real comfort but I did have the opportunity to acquire fifty-nine chamber pots when the guards' hostel was closed during my time as assistant yardmaster at Temple Mills, Stratford. Properly planted they would have graced any garden.

BRITANNIA BRIDGE DRAMA

The dramatic 1970 fire on the bridge over the Menai Strait had many repercussions, as Brian Arbon relates

I had only been the assistant shipping and port manager at Holyhead for a few months when I took a phone call at home during the evening of Saturday 23 May 1970. It was from the shift manager at the port who said that there was smoke coming from the Britannia Bridge, which ran over the Menai Strait, and the Down mail train had been cautioned, but there was nothing to worry about.

BR shipping services and the railway ports had only recently been detached from railway regional control and combined into a new and separate Shipping and International Services division. Whilst it concerned us at Holyhead, a 'minor' fire on the railway was the responsibility of the divisional organisation at Stoke, not us. So I went to bed and slept undisturbed.

The next morning, Whit Sunday in those days, the fire was the first item on the national television news. Robert Stephenson's wrought-iron tubular bridge, which had carried trains between Anglesey and the mainland since 1850, had been put out of service by a raging fire. How could a metal bridge burn so fiercely? Trains ran across the bridge in tubes, which were rectangular in section and fabricated from wrought-iron plates riveted together. These would not have burned but, to protect the flat tops of the two tubes, later engineers had built a pitched timber roof over the whole length of each tube. Even later engineers had periodically coated this with tar, allowing the flames to roar through the void beneath.

Despite the best efforts of the Caernarfonshire and Anglesey fire brigades, the bridge's height and construction and the lack of an adequate water supply meant they were unable to control the fire, which spread all the way across from the mainland to the Anglesey side. The fierce heat caused the wrought-iron plates to expand and rupture at the rivet holes. This weakened the bridge and initially it was feared that the tubes might collapse into the Menai Strait below. It subsequently turned out that the fire was accidentally started by boys trying to smoke-out roosting pigeons.

An official LNWR illustration of Robert Stephenson's original Britannia Bridge of 1850.

And to think I slept through all that! Once I took in the BBC News I hurried to the port to find that the overnight passengers to and from Ireland had been dealt with and things were at something of a standstill whilst everyone involved worked out what to do next.

The wires must have been buzzing between our shipping division in London and the railway divisional office in Stoke and all levels above, but for the next few hours I fielded calls from one journalist after another wanting to know what we were doing and intended doing.

The immediate first move was to transfer the Dun Laoghaire passenger ships to operate from Heysham and divert the London boat trains there. This was not so long after the Beeching Report and, given the obvious huge cost of repairing the bridge, the immediate fear of the strongly unionised workforce was that the railway across Anglesey might be closed for good and employment at Holyhead greatly reduced. So they wheeled out their big guns.

The local MP, Cledwyn Hughes, was Minister of Agriculture and in the Cabinet. His constituency agent was a member of our clerical local departmental committee (LDC). Three of the four members of the dockers' LDC were town councillors and two of them were also county councillors.

That Sunday they were also busy planning. A very high-powered visit to the bridge was organised for the next day, Whit Monday, with three Cabinet ministers present. George ('Order! Order!') Thomas, Secretary of State for Wales, and Fred Mulley, the Minister of Transport, flew in to nearby RAF Valley; I'm not sure whether Hughes came with them or was already home for the weekend. My boss, the shipping and port manager, was ordered to be there as part of the welcoming party but later found it impossible, in his venerable Wolseley, to keep up with the police-escorted high-speed convoy on the way back to Holyhead.

A 'town meeting' had been hastily arranged for the evening at the British Railways Staff Association (BRSA) Club and the National Union of Railwaymen branch chairman was able to assure everyone in the packed hall, to great acclaim, that there had been conversations with Downing Street (where Harold Wilson was destined to have just nineteen more days in office). The bridge would be repaired and as a result Holyhead's future as a railway port was guaranteed. In such secretive ways are major decisions often taken, but at least we knew where we stood.

Holyhead, and indeed Anglesey, was cut off from the rest of the railway network system for over a year and a half until the bridge reopened as a speed-restricted single line on 30 January 1972. Early on during that period the stranded locomotives were taken back to the mainland on low-loader lorries. They passed close in front of the Edinburgh Castle pub, just outside the dock gate, to the shocked amazement of one late-lunchtime drinker who staggered out just as a main-line diesel passed right in front of him!

The Irish passenger services continued to operate at Heysham, but the car ferry was unaffected, as Anglesey still had one mainland connection over Telford's suspension bridge, which opened for horse-drawn traffic in 1826. In an effort to retain as much rail traffic as possible, cattle and containers were moved by road over this vulnerable link to improvised railheads at Menai Bridge and Caernarfon where, fortunately, the redundant tracks had not been lifted. I was able to walk across the main bridge on top of the tubes and saw for myself just how much damage had been done by such a relatively trivial action.

Meanwhile, at Holyhead, a major project to introduce an ISO container service across the Irish Sea was under way. The plan was to build a new berth with two ship-to-shore container cranes and an adjacent Freightliner terminal, also with two cranes. This was to be the principal transfer location between the new port terminals in Dublin and Belfast and the Freightliner depots at Willesden, Birmingham and Manchester Trafford Park. The maritime link would be provided by two new cellular container ships: the MV *Rhodri Mawr* and the MV *Brian Boroime*.

The enforced lull in activities enabled us to reorganise and retrain the staff as crane and lorry drivers to operate the whole shebang. Quite a few who did not feel up to these new tasks took voluntary redundancy. We also used this slack time to invite Freightliner staff from the terminals we would be serving to come and see us and get to know the people they would be in daily communication with once the Britannia Bridge reopened.

To celebrate the reopening, the first mail boat to sail back into Holyhead was greeted by fireworks and the town band at 12.15 a.m., with a temperature of –10 degrees, the spittle freezing in the musicians' instruments as they waited to strike up; a rather different extreme to the bridge inferno.

ANGLIA TRAIN PLANNERS

————◀◯▶————

Chris Blackman's search for timetable information revealed just how knowledgeable train planning staff could be

As operations planning manager for the Anglia Region, I soon discovered that the train planning staff there were a knowledgeable crew. Chris Hurricks was the principal timetable planner for the Liverpool Street–Norwich main line and branches, which included the line to Harwich ('for the Continent'); indeed, his encyclopaedic knowledge seemed to stretch right across Europe as well.

Late one Friday afternoon I was clearing my desk in preparation for a week's holiday in the Jura, and had it in mind to take the family for a day trip to Geneva in Switzerland and possibly up a mountain rack-railway line. I went to consult the Cook's European timetable kept in one of the office cupboards, only to find it was locked. I looked around at the handful of staff still in the office.

'I want to consult the Cook's timetable. Has anyone got the key?'

'Terry has, but, oh, he's on leave this afternoon.'

Then, from the far end of the office, Chris Hurricks sidled up to me. 'Can I help?'

I explained briefly what I wanted to know. Chris contemplated for a moment, and then advised that, if we were staying in the Jura, rather than drive to Geneva, it would be better to drive to the station at Nyon which was on the main line from Geneva and had plenty of car-parking spaces. From there

I could catch one of the trains that ran every half-hour to Lausanne. Alternate trains went on to Montreux from where I could change to the narrow-gauge rack-and-pinion line up the Rochers-de-Naye mountain. At Montreux, he explained, the change would be easy to do because the narrow-gauge trains went from an adjacent platform. Moreover, I would not need to go up to the booking hall as there was a very convenient ticket office for the narrow-gauge trains on that very platform. He added that trains ran up the mountain every hour, with a connection off the train from Nyon. For good measure he gave me details of the time of departure of the direct train from Nyon to connect with the narrow gauge. Finally, he told me, quite accurately as it turned out, the price of coffee at the station at the top of the mountain.

This was twenty-five years ago – information provided quicker than I could have obtained today from the Internet. Never underestimate quiet professionalism or the degree and breadth of staff knowledge!

A LESSON TO BE REMEMBERED

————◄o►————

Jim Dorward tells of a derailment that contained some
valuable lessons

It is Thursday 13 March 1958. I am with a very experienced permanent-way engineer on the 8.21 a.m. from Perth to Edinburgh (Waverley) via Kinross Junction, travelling as far as Dunfermline (Lower) where we will change on to another train to travel further up the line to Inverkeithing.

My companion points out that this arrangement enables our original train to run through Inverkeithing without a stop, giving it a good run at the 1 in 70 rising gradient between there and the Forth Bridge. He adds that the value of this piece of train planning was underlined by an incident on Sunday 7 March 1954 when he and others from the Perth district engineer's office were involved in the matter of a serious accident on the gradient.

The accident involved Class A4 4-6-2 No. 60027 *Kingfisher* while in charge of 'The Aberdonian' – the thirteen-coach 6.55 p.m. Aberdeen–London (King's Cross). On this occasion the engine had considerable difficulty in battling with the gradient. Inside North Queensferry Tunnel, with the A4's driving wheels spinning, the driver thought his train was moving forward slowly, but this was only an impression – the tunnel being full of noise and smoke – it was, in fact, almost stationary. The noise in the confined space must have seemed horrendous, making it extremely difficult to make a judgement about progress. Then, unknown to the driver, with the driving wheels still spinning, the heavy train actually started to move backwards down the gradient towards a set of catch points just outside the tunnel mouth. These points were, of course, there to deal with any runaway and thereby prevent a collision with another train.

The engineer then got to the reason behind his story. He said that the track had been renewed during an 'Engineer's Possession' of the line, resulting in two significant features. First of all, the slightly curved top of the new bullhead rails gave a smaller contact area, about the size of a thumbnail, under each of the A4's six driving wheels, giving lower than normal adhesion. This was exacerbated by the loss of momentum when the train had braked slightly for the 20mph temporary speed restriction covering the new track. Secondly, the catch points had been clamped in the non-derailing position during the renewal work. After the clamps were removed, the slide chairs had to be cleaned and oiled before the line was reopened to traffic.

Probably as a result of the last coach of 'The Aberdonian' passing through the catch points in the normal direction at less than walking speed, and before the

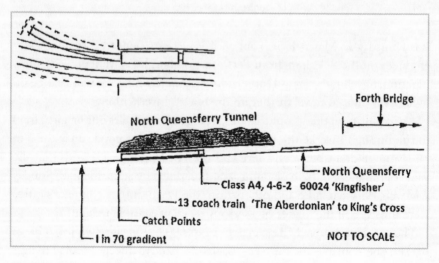

The North Queensferry Tunnel incident. (Jim Dorward)

train started to slide back, the spring in the catch points was not strong enough to return the switch blades completely to the derailing position. Consequently, when the leading bogie of the now-slipping train returned to the points, this time in the facing direction, it was able to slip through a small gap between the switch and stock rails, thereby failing to head towards the buffer stop at the end of the short catch siding and remaining on the main line instead.

The passage of this leading bogie must have nudged the spring into full operation, causing the second bogie to take the route into the siding. Not surprisingly, with the coach now moving along two different routes, a significant derailment became inevitable, and duly occurred, involving the last three coaches of the train.

The engineer then stressed the point of the lesson to me: the need to observe the operation of catch points by the first train to pass over them after track work if there was any doubt about them being able to function properly.

In his accident report on the *Kingfisher* incident, Brigadier Langley of Her Majesty's Railway Inspectorate recommended the provision of marker lights in both North Queensferry and Inverkeithing tunnels to enable drivers to establish their direction of travel when the driving wheels are slipping and the tunnels are filled with smoke and steam.

About twenty years later, this lesson passed on to me during the train journey to Dunfermline flashed into my brain when, as an area civil engineer, I was told that the first bogie of a DMU travelling in the wrong direction had failed to derail at a set of catch points at Barrhead. My record of this incident appeared on page 108 of an earlier volume entitled *Signal Box Coming Up, Sir.*

ONE WAY ONLY

———◦———

For railways, some pigeons were a nuisance while others, as Jim Dorward and Bill Parker experienced, represented revenue

Jim Dorward recalls a day in 1957 when he observed a special train waiting to depart from Larbert at 11.10 a.m. Its passengers were doubtless apprehensive of the day ahead, as they only had single tickets and would be expected to find their own way home! This was because these passengers were pigeons, new to the sport of racing and on a training exercise.

The train consisted of two converted bogie brake vans fitted with shelving to house the pigeon baskets. Demand for this service could be high so the specials were scheduled to run Monday to Thursday until further notice, and subject to demand. The train would collect more 'passengers' at Coatbridge Central, Motherwell, Wishaw Central, Law Junction, Carluke, Carstairs, Thankerton, Symington, Lamington, Abington and Crawford before terminating at Elvanfoot at 1.56 p.m. There, the birds would be released from their hampers and the time recorded so that the owners could work out the flight speed by comparing it with the time their birds arrived home. The special would run round and return to Larbert at 3 p.m., dropping the empty baskets on the way.

As the crow flies – and assuming pigeons have the same navigational equipment as crows – the pigeons would manage the 50-mile journey fast enough to beat the train home!

Bill Parker was involved in the pigeon business at the receiving end in Mexborough where his father was stationmaster and where the arrangements were somewhat different to those in Scotland. The pigeon specials were quite frequent weekend events, he recalls. A train of three or more pigeon vans with a coach for the bird owners and the organisers would arrive on Saturday evenings in time for the passengers, some of whom were making a weekend holiday of it, to get to the pubs before closing time. One member of the party would remain in the train for security purposes.

Each train was stabled overnight in the goods yard and moved into the east end of the Up platform quite early on the Sunday morning. It was placed as far away from the station buildings as practical for the next operation – of unloading the baskets on to the platform under the supervision of the station foreman and the pigeon fanciers. The continuous noise of hundreds of squawking pigeons was horrendously loud and nerve racking, even in the stationmaster's house from which the lounge and an upstairs bedroom looked out on to the platform.

My father wisely left the opening of the baskets to the station foreman, himself a pigeon fancier, and concentrated on SLW over the Down line and on the passengers. With the help of a couple of hefty BTP officers, these and many onlookers behind a barrier were kept well away from the main hive of activity.

The opening of the baskets and discharge of their occupants was under very strict discipline; I had what the fanciers regarded as a very important role. Armed with a clipboard containing a large number of their official forms, I had to check and record the departure times of batches of pigeons, basket by basket, aiming for complete accuracy, not just to the minute but to the second! I was carefully overseen by one or more of the fanciers but, despite being meticulous in my recording, there were always arguments and comments like, 'Get your eyes tested, lad.'

I was well prepared for both event and behaviour. Having only recently completed my National Service as a senior NCO, I wore my army uniform, plus steel helmet and wellies, partly to give myself a little prestige and partly as protection against the dive-bombing antics of some of the birds.

It was all a hectic, noisy affair with the fanciers' enthusiasm for their birds and interests making them somewhat over-eager to ensure things went well and that their own pigeons were not disadvantaged. On the whole, however, they were very jolly and friendly chaps. The goodwill in evidence did not extend to my mother, however, whose house windows were badly fouled by the pigeons but, as a railwayman's wife, she was well equipped to cope with any railway-associated activity.

Whether the pigeon business made money is questionable, but for me it was fun and it gave me a useful insight into the behavioural attitudes of people when there is a strong determination to win.

PUTTING ON A SHOW

———◦———

Mike Lamport records two examples of how public relations helped to show the railway in a positive light

The opening ceremony of the new Stansted Airport terminal by Her Majesty the Queen took place on Friday 15 March 1991. It was planned with military precision, not only because it was going to be shown live on BBC television, but also because it had been agreed that the royal party would travel, not by royal train, but by our Stansted Express train from Liverpool Street. The train could not run late.

In fact, it ran like clockwork and the two Class 322 units in their grey and green livery and shadowed by the BBC and police helicopters arrived almost to the second at the brand-new Stansted Airport station in the chilly undercroft of the terminal.

The royal party was travelling in the rear unit of the otherwise empty train and I had carefully placed the reception line of dignitaries in the exact spot at which the rearmost set of sliding doors would stop. All of the preparations and measurements paid off and we were spot on in our assessment. However, there was a painful pause of a few seconds while we waited anxiously for the driver to release the doors and then for the orange sidelights to be illuminated.

There we all stood – the Lord Lieutenant, British Airports Authority and BR dignitaries and local worthies – but nothing happened. We could see Her Majesty standing in the vestibule alongside the red-waistcoated royal train steward, but they too seemed to be waiting for something to happen.

Then it dawned on me. In all the weeks of planning and rehearsal for this groundbreaking journey by a sliding-door train, we never considered the question of who was going to press the passenger-operated door button inside the train. Against all protocol I broke ranks and, leaning as far as I could without blocking the BBC's live camera view, I pressed the door button on the outside of the train and quickly drew back into the throng as the beaming monarch stepped down on to the platform to a great cheer and the prearranged musical fanfare from the Essex school orchestra.

Sir Bob Reid then invited Her Majesty to step up on to the rostrum and say a few words before pulling the cord to unveil not one but two plaques, both of which read 'Stansted Airport Station opened by Her Majesty the Queen on Friday 15th March 1991', with the words 'Network South East' along the bottom. The giant background plaque, which I had designed to fill a void and to act as a windbreak in that cavernous station, provided Her Majesty with a relatively warm spot in a uniformly cold place and was legible on the live BBC coverage compered by the incomparable Richard Baker.

The Stansted Express operation was managed by Network South East's newly constituted West Anglia & Great Northern Train Operating Unit, of which I was public affairs manager. It straddled the boundary of the former Anglia and Eastern regions and it was in these borderlands that I discovered the 'Fiefdom of West Anglia'.

This 'mini state' had managed to maintain some sort of independence while the two BR regions were concentrating on tearing themselves apart, and was the province of Area Manager Stuart Davies and his team. I quickly discovered that they had a very 'can do' attitude, particularly when it came to organising events.

One of Stuart's team was railwayman and local councillor John Boothroyd, who was ably supported by operations chief Brian Heath; they were the driving force behind the phenomenon that was the Cambridge 'Gala' Days. These annual events were held during the last weekend of the school summer holidays in disused sidings, which later became part of the track of the controversial Cambridge Guided Busway. Locomotives and stock were put on display, sideshows arranged and stalls erected, and all proceeds went to local charities.

To give a flavour of the scale of these events, the line-up for the 1991 Gala included a Class 303 Glasgow Blue Train shuttling visitors from Cambridge to Stansted Airport and back, the Romney, Hythe & Dymchurch Railway's Green Goddess giving rides on a specially laid length of 15in-gauge track at King's Lynn and the naming of not one but two new diesel locomotives – Class 59 *Village of Great Elm* and Class 60 *Robert Adam*. There were also special trains on the former Cambridge–St Ives and King's Lynn–Middleton Towers freight-only branches formed of Class 310 EMUs topped and tailed by Class 31 and 37 locomotives.

This was not all. At the same time, this resourceful team was also pulling together what we thought would be the last opportunity to ride behind steam traction on the Cambridge–King's Lynn line, viz. the Fenline Steam Weekend to be held on 19–20 October 1991. This major undertaking saw in action No. 4472 *Flying Scotsman*, No. 34027 *Taw Valley* and the former local locomotive No. 70000 *Britannia*. Between them they provided a programme of regular trips throughout the weekend, attracting enthusiasts and local people to the line and to our message: 'Say goodbye to the past and look forward to a bright, electrified future.'

I was delighted with the media coverage that this 'last ever' opportunity created, and Anglia Television even allocated a crew to join Brian on a trial run, which *Flying Scotsman* made to King's Lynn and back in the preceding week. This footage was quietly interspersed with the actual day's shoot and produced an excellent piece of reportage. What they didn't show, Brian told me, was the Thursday's encounter with a 'Fen Blow' – a fenland phenomenon that sees dry earth whipped up off the empty, flat landscape into a cloud, which then deposits its contents wherever it chooses. In this case it was over what is arguably the most famous steam locomotive in the world.

These events all enabled visitors to see for themselves the work already undertaken to prepare the line for electrification, part of my job of keeping opinion formers up to date with what turned out to be a rather more protracted process than we had planned for.

One of our chief allies in this period was West Norfolk MP Henry Bellingham. He was a guest of ours at the 1991 King's Lynn Festival where Network South East was the principal sponsor, and I clearly remember standing with him in King's Lynn's famous Tuesday Market Place while, in the fading light of a July evening, my boss Chris Green mapped out his vision for the 'Thameslink 2000' on a piece of paper resting on the bonnet of a parked car.

After the demise of Network South East, I took it upon myself to continue to support the festival by sponsoring at least one headline concert each year. We were able to keep in touch with the opinion formers in an area where the Borough Council of King's Lynn and West Norfolk had shown commendable foresight and commitment by signing a unique agreement with BR that secured electrification.

The agreement guaranteed to make up for the loss to BR if the electrification of the line failed to bring the expected revenue boost. In the event, this support was never needed because the service quickly attracted new customers and succeeded in enticing back many of the former regulars, who had found other ways of travelling during the three years since the withdrawal of the locomotive-hauled through trains and their substitution by a much slower and less convenient DMU shuttle service connecting at Cambridge with London trains.

Concerns over the revised layout at Ely North Junction following the Bellshill single-lead accident were still delaying us from announcing a start date for electrified services; nonetheless, we had to go ahead with preparation for a royal event to celebrate the scheme, even though, as the media was quick to point out, we didn't yet have an electrified railway to show off to our royal guest of honour – Her Majesty the Queen Mother, who had graciously agreed to perform the naming of EMU No. 317361 *King's Lynn Festival* in her role as its patron.

The day for the big event dawned, a gloriously warm and sunny 28 July, and we all gathered at King's Lynn for the occasion, along with BR chairman Sir Bob Reid, who had travelled up from London that morning.

At 11.30 a.m. on the dot, Her Majesty stepped from the royal car on to the red carpet where she was introduced to the official party before Sir Bob invited her to unveil the red and silver nameplate. As the photographers snapped away and the television cameras whirred, Sir Bob sought to lead Her Majesty to where the 100 or so invited guests were awaiting her arrival in a marquee for lunch. But this well-travelled lady had other ideas.

Suddenly Sir Bob beckoned me to his side and whispered that Her Majesty had asked to look inside the train. This was an eventuality that we had not prepared for but, of course, had to agree to, even though it required me to forego years of maintaining royal etiquette by taking Her Majesty's right arm while Sir Bob, with his one arm, took her left arm to gently aid her up the step and into the train. Then, while she and Sir Bob chatted happily away in the small first-class section of the train, I withdrew to the platform in order to manage the potential ramifications of this change to the, as ever, carefully choreographed and forensically timed programme. Mercifully, after just 2 or 3 minutes the two emerged and Sir Bob escorted the royal visitor to the marquee.

After lunch and the departure of our royal guest, Sir Bob told me that while they had chatted in the train the Queen Mother had told him that as a child the Bowes-Lyon family used to travel on the Orient Express, which – unlike our train – had tables on which she had very much enjoyed writing and drawing. I made a note that any new trains on this 'royal route' ought to be equipped with tables!

Electrification was an immediate success and, by working closely with our civic partners and the Fen Line Users Association (led by its pragmatic new chairman Robert Stripe), we were quickly and without controversy able to tweak the service to meet emerging demands. In the longer term, however, we were both looking forward to new trains – the Class 365 Networker Expresses, along with their royally decreed tables!

A LONELY FUNERAL

———◄○►———

Colin Driver describes just one of the many ongoing complications that tended to characterise large depots

At the large Southern Region goods depot, where I was the goods agent, at least one of the goods sheds had staff working at night, and any disputes were often discussed in the morning. One senior foreman was used to having his judgement questioned, despite an almost 100 per cent record of correct decisions.

One morning, I was met with the sad news that the foreman in question had died during the night. When the LDC said they wanted a discussion about the supervisor, I was able to say that they were 'too late'. However, they were aware of the sudden death and had wanted to discuss the number of staff that would be released to attend the funeral, and their pay.

It was a tradition in parts of London that staff would line the route of the funeral cortege. In this case I was asked to agree to release a large number of staff (the depot employed over 1,100 men) and give them basic pay plus the average tonnage bonus. The members of staff who stayed at work wanted extra bonus for the tonnage they handled, but this would have been inordinately expensive.

A simple solution was offered involving a small number of staff and no extra bonus, which inevitably was refused by the LDC. The proposals did eventually form the basis for an agreement, but with dire consequences forecast for my own funeral.

It was claimed that I could be the first London goods agent within living memory not to have any staff attending his funeral. I was able to say that if this were the case, I would go with a smile on my face!

IN THE BLEAK MIDWINTER

———◄○►———

A severe winter meant a lot of problems for David Barraclough's
Boston goods depot

The land around Boston is flat and fruitful. Two crops a year is commonplace, with some places happily manage more. Summer is glorious in East Lincolnshire but in winter, all too often, the wind comes straight from the Urals, nothing impeding it en route. The winter of 1962–63 proved this point.

The Boston goods yard at that time was quite extensive, with several single-storey buildings dotted about, a shed, an office, three small brick 'huts' and a three-storey warehouse in the south-west corner. A small marshalling yard, four running lines and up to fifteen scattered sidings, plus a 14-acre BR-owned orchard gave little protection from any weather. The yard abutted against the London Road and then came the River Witham and the expanse of the municipally owned Boston Dock, with warehouses along the eastern quay, more sidings scattered about, hydraulic cranes, a coaling hoist and a three-storey granary tucked away in a corner by the river. Rail access to and from the dock was by level crossing over the London Road and then by a railway swing bridge with a tiny signal box and a BR rowing boat fastened to the riverbank below. As goods agent at Boston this was my patch, together with a large staff that included clerks, supervisors, dock labourers, lorry drivers and guards.

Shunting and pilot work in the yard, sidings, dock and station was undertaken by a three-shift yard pilot, a two-shift dock and transfer pilot and a single-shift Monday-to-Friday pilot – all Barclay 0-6-0 locomotives. There was also a Class 03 Sleaford pilot that served the stations at Hubberts Bridge, Swineshead and Heckington.

By the end of each September the evenings at Boston began to get cold and, in 1962, I donned wellington boots and thick socks for daily work, never abandoning them until the end of March 1963. By early October night-time frosts were regularly severe. To avoid damage to our seven road lorries we arranged for a shunter with a road-vehicle licence to start up each vehicle for half an hour every 2 hours. In the worst conditions this was increased to running vehicles every other hour and even continuously. There were some

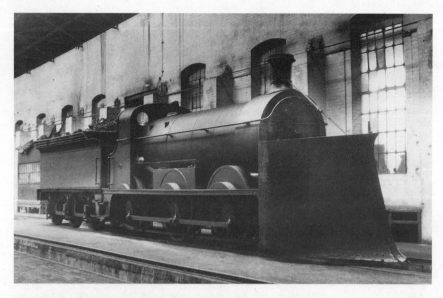

For much of railway history the clearance of heavy snow from the line was undertaken by charging the blockage with this sort of snowplough, aided by hard work with the humble shovel.

complaints that this should have been a job for the regular lorry drivers on overtime, but then, we pointed out, who would drive their vehicles during the day? The nearest other BR delivery vehicles were in the Nottingham area, but somehow we managed to serve the large parts of south Lincolnshire in between throughout the winter.

Whilst many parts of the UK had several feet of snow during that winter, a couple of inches was the most we had – the east wind saw to that. Ice was another matter. Lincolnshire has many miles of deep, often wide, drainage channels, the largest of which can be up to 20ft wide. These drains froze early on, some spectacularly. In places there was ice 16ft thick up to the top of the banks but with running water right down at the bottom.

By mid December the River Witham and the adjacent dock were completely frozen over with ice thick enough to prevent access by ships of any size. One of the last to arrive was carrying a cargo of pig iron, and some of the unloading dockers threw ingots over the side to see if the ice would break. It didn't and the ingots then had to be rescued and loaded properly into their waiting wagon.

The very low temperatures kept the River Witham frozen, which helped the competitive skating that took place near Spalding, with some of the best races for many years taking place in January 1963. Here at Boston a notable event was the trip made by some local lads in a Land Rover on the river from just north of the Grand Sluice to Woodhall station, nearly 18 miles each way.

Despite the difficulties, the railway kept going throughout the winter. Our locomotive shed had closed in the October, with most of the remaining steam turns now being served by incoming locomotives. For two turns, however, engines came light from New England yard at Peterborough. On one particular evening, the 2-6-0 making the 32-mile run tender first had to stop near Kirton and throw out the fire, as the water in the tender had frozen solid. One of our diesel pilots had to be despatched to the rescue.

On the positive side, we were still operational while in many parts of England conditions were such that road haulage had become impossible. Snow in the south-west, basically anywhere beyond Bristol, was especially bad. One of Boston's regular services was the 4V25 8 p.m. Boston–Stoke Gifford fitted freight. For much of January and February 1963 this train not only ran every night (except Saturdays) with a full load of fifty-five wagons, but sometimes there was a second service and even a third, depending on what traffic had found its way into Boston from the rest of Lincolnshire and what help we could get from New England yard. The special interest of one of the assistant yardmasters there did much to enable us to keep this vital flow moving, further aided by the agreement of the Exeter goods agent to take traffic for the south-west on the 4V25.

This was the time when railway communication was still supposed to be routed via one's district office, but I had found it useful to build up a network of contacts with other goods agents and stationmasters at places as far apart as Edinburgh (Waverley) and Merthyr Tydfil. These contacts proved vital in keeping traffic moving and in carrying out some of our more imaginative plans.

For some time we sent Merthyr Tydfil a weekly AF insulated container load of frozen chickens. This travelled by freight service to Lincoln, thence on the Tamworth Mail, forward ECS to Birmingham New Street, then passenger train on to Cardiff from whence the container became 'tail traffic' for the first passenger service up the valley to Merthyr. All went well until the commercial people at Lincoln district office learned that the movement was at freight rates, despite the passenger service element. Passenger rates were too expensive and we lost the traffic.

We had more success with the same firm's frozen-food container movements to London and the south. The evening fish train from New Clee (Grimsby)–King's Cross stopped at the station for a Boston crew to take over from the Immingham men, with the engine then taking water at the yard. While it was doing so we took the opportunity to use the Boston yard pilot to add our containers at the rear.

And thus we survived a nasty winter, keeping traffic moving when the odds were often against us, and looking forward to the return of better weather and rather more normality.

BACK TO NORMAL

──────◄○►──────

Winter over and Boston returned to normal. Not that life was dull,
as David Barraclough makes clear

Towards the end of March 1963 the weather and temperature began to improve. The ice covering the dock surface was broken up one afternoon by an arriving vessel, and over the next fortnight normal working at the dock resumed. During this period we took the opportunity to thaw out two dozen or so wagons of 'washed smalls' – export coal for German power stations. They were moved close to the coal hoist and well away from the usual vast stock of imported Baltic and Russian timber so that small fires could be lit underneath the wagons while our dock labourers applied lump hammers to the wagon sides and underframe to help the loosening-up process.

Very soon all normal, regular dock arrivals resumed. A Geest boat, and occasionally two, arrived on every tide with market vegetables and fruit from Maassluis in Holland. These vessels often took back live cattle that had either arrived by rail into our own lairage or come by road into the Buitelaar lairage. Another regular vessel was the owner captain's 350-ton MV *Fiducia*, which arrived twice weekly whatever the North Sea weather, again with agricultural produce.

During the long winter, quantities of timber had built up in Scandinavia and by April the Midlands urgently needed supplies. Rail forwardings were made in Ashworth Kirk private-owner wagons or in Hyfits to a consignee in Leicester who spread his intake by giving us half his tonnage and taking the remainder in barges travelling to their destination via the River Witham, the Fossdyke navigation, the River Trent and then the River Soar.

Other regular Boston Dock arrivals were fertiliser in bulk for Saxilby and gypsum from Sardinia by the aged 1916 vessel MV *Giannas*, destined for East Leake and Tetbury. For these flows we used 16-ton mineral wagons that had arrived with export coal. After the coal had been tipped at the coal hoist, BR dock labourers swept the wagons out and then reloaded and sheeted. A similar process, minus the sheeting, applied to the imported pig iron.

We had sugar-beet factories close by at Bardney and Spalding and used the same 16-ton mineral wagons for these forwardings during the annual autumn sugar-beet 'campaign'. Road-vehicle queues at the factories meant that farmers might only manage one load a day with direct road delivery, whereas bringing the beet into our depot and using a single elevator meant that some 750 tons could be put on rail. The same situation applied to malting barley, which was also conveyor loaded, this time to bulk-grain vans which were then positioned as required by the yard pilot, checked by the carriage and wagon examiner and duly sent off to Scotland, Silloth or, occasionally, Snape in East Anglia.

Reinforcing rod was regularly imported through Boston. It had been brought down the Rhine by barge, transhipped in Holland and then carried across the North Sea for unloading at Boston on to waiting bogie bolster wagons, often purloined from passing New England–Frodingham services. After weighing and customs clearance the rods went forward to Sutton-in-Ashfield by our two daily services through Colwick yard. How, I wondered, could such cheap material stand the colossal transport costs of such a series of journeys? And pig-iron forwardings from Boston Dock continue even now, with up to four trains a week being despatched in covered steel carriers.

Sundries (small-goods consignments) were the subject of a BR decision in late 1964 designed to reduce costs. Wagons of sundries traffic would have to convey at least 1.5 tons of revenue traffic to a specific set of destinations or empty wagons would not be supplied. In Lincolnshire there were five of us – at Grimsby, Louth, Boston, Spalding and Lincoln. How could we comply with these new instructions? We got together and quickly decided how to address the problem. Using the existing pattern of pick-up freight services it was easy for Grimsby to start the load for a wagon that could be added to at Louth and Boston and still depart within 24 hours of loading for station groups covering King's Cross, East Anglia, some Midlands areas, Scotland and the West Country. For other destinations better served by Lincoln or Grimsby a wagon could be started at Boston or Louth and added to in the same way, while Spalding could route via Lincoln, if necessary, although their sundries business was not great.

As a result of this enterprise we assembled a list of thirty-five destinations to which we could guarantee to load 1.5 tons per wagon on specified days in the week. The arrangements worked and we lost no business; however, there were internal inquiries about how we could have achieved these results – there were even unannounced inspections of the books – but we all passed with flying colours.

An earlier scheme to improve local loadings had produced mixed results. The boxed fruit, vegetables and flowers dealt with at Spalding would no longer be carted, but a special rate of £70 per van would be offered for consignments brought into the forwarding station and collected at the other end, however much or little was loaded into it. The scheme proved a tremendous success, but when applied to the fish traffic from Hull and Grimsby, which had often loaded poorly, it was not taken up because the merchants were not prepared to have each other's boxes in the same van. The story was different again at Mallaig where for years a BG vehicle was loaded every day with iced boxes of fish and was conveyed to London on the overnight sleeper.

SEASIDE SUMMER

———◦———

TA training over, Geoff Body's first supernumerary appointment was at the seaside

After nearly two and a half years of absorbing information I was tired of being a pupil and looked forward to putting into practice the things I had learned during my experiences as a TA. Information on my first post-training appointment was eagerly awaited and duly arrived: I was to spend the summer of 1958 as supernumerary assistant stationmaster at Clacton-on-Sea. I was pleased, not only because of the extra experience this would provide in dealing with intensive passenger business, but also because I could find local accommodation that would allow my wife and two young sons to join me – some compensation for the long periods spent away from home during my training.

Clacton was a pretty straightforward terminus with four platforms (each with engine release points) and a generous frontage and booking area. I found Stationmaster Dick Dennis rather inscrutable initially, but learned to both respect and like him. My first few days were pretty routine. One of the main tasks was to prepare for the hectic Saturdays (a feature of Clacton) and for when a lot of extra trains brought thousands of holidaymakers to the town and its Butlin's holiday camp in the nearby village of Jaywick. A key factor in the Saturday mayhem was to check that everything – locomotives, stock, drivers, guards etc. – arrived when it should and to know exactly what it was booked to do next.

We did all we could to prepare for each manic Saturday. A sales representative went along to Butlin's a couple of days beforehand to make as many advance bookings as possible in order to relieve the pressure on our own booking office. There would still be a queue several hundred yards long outside the station from quite early on, everyone with a week's luggage and their own special needs and queries. The assistant stationmaster handled many of the queries: lost children, people without funds, wrong luggage and so on.

Inside, we anxiously awaited the first train of the day, a special from the Midlands via the Colne Valley line and Colchester. Somehow, if this service arrived on time it augured well for the rest of the day, but any one of a dozen disappointments might be revealed – locomotive mechanical problems, crew who did not know the road for their next working or did not want to work the overtime necessary to perform it. Then it was improvisation time – finding an alternative, often 'robbing Peter to pay Paul' by taking a guard from a later job and then having to fill the subsequent gap. Diesels were just appearing at this time and there was more than one occasion when a driver just did not have that know-how which comes with familiarity to remedy a fault, so a steam replacement had to be conjured up from the shed.

If all went well, arriving train engines would get released to go to the shed and take water and the departing engine could back on to the train for its next working. Alternatively, the shed pilot would take the empty stock to the carriage sidings until it was required to go back into the station. Some basic interior cleaning was done but this was greatly limited by the time between stock arrival and departure.

We checked with each crew member that he knew when his next working was, made sure he knew where the mess room was and then checked he was fully available as each departure time neared.

All this took place amid hordes of passengers arriving and departing, all seemingly unsure about something and needing to be guided or advised. We had no train announcing system, just slat destination boards, something I remember well as a result of having carelessly ordered 'more sluts for the platform' from the Stratford stores.

Dick Dennis took a few days off on one occasion, leaving me in charge – no great risk, as the station inspectors were an able lot – but, as is the way of things, there was a coach derailment in the carriage sidings. After inspecting what appeared to be something of a mess I rang Stratford suggesting we needed the breakdown crane. Wiser heads than mine sent a breakdown van and treated me to the spectacle of how easy experienced professionals could make a re-railing seem just with the clever use of ramps and a careful driver.

By Saturday evening I was always tired beyond exhaustion, but Clacton on a Saturday was a useful and interesting experience. It was calmer during the week but Sundays brought a lot of day-trippers and there was a lot of activity connected with the advancing electrification of the line. Youngsters were encouraged to become 'Progress Chasers' and take an interest in how

The hectic summer seaside activity became even harder for railways to handle in bad weather like this at Skegness where two trains wait for their quota of homeward-bound holidaymakers.

the electrification construction work was going, while the introduction of an Essex Coast Express meant another occasion for pretty hostesses, media coverage and a lot of background work for the station staff.

In personal terms, through the kindness of friends, we had the use of a beach hut at Holland-on-Sea so that when I was not working there was an opportunity for some family seaside relaxation. My eventual move on to Temple Mills marshalling yard would prove something of a contrast.

RESERVATION CHALLENGES

———◄o►———

Like Geoff Body in the previous 'Seaside Summer' piece, his son Ian also experienced the pressures holiday traffic brought

For the summer of 1974 I left my management training and took on the seasonal role of stationmaster at Paignton. It covered the three stations of Torre, Torquay and Paignton, together with the coaching stock stabling and turnround cleaning yard at Goodrington. As far as workload was concerned it was decidedly unbalanced.

Mondays were spent recovering from the hectic weekend while Tuesdays, Wednesdays and Thursdays involved little more than station and signal box visits, booking office checks and maintaining good working relations with the staff. Friday morning was the lull before the storm and that duly began in the late afternoon.

It was at this point that empty coaching stock (ECS) began to arrive at Newton Abbot and Paignton to form the morning services to the Midlands and the north; the reservation labels to accompany them came separately. With the considerable pressure on available seating accommodation, every train was fully reserved and every seat had to be individually labelled so that it could be identified by passengers joining the train on the following day.

With a minimum of six services involved at this stage and each conveying at least ten passenger-carrying vehicles of sixty-four seats per vehicle, there were just under 4,000 seats to be labelled. Each label had to be fixed underneath a retaining screw that had to be undone and then retightened.

This fixing process was in itself a time challenge, but additionally there was always the threat of an Eastern or Midland region 'three-a-side' coach covering a Western 'four-a-side' working. With the former normally configured to accommodate six passengers in each compartment and the latter eight, this would mean that eight reservation labels per compartment had to be accommodated within a compartment with only six seating numbers – a recipe for confusion.

The 'high tech' solution for this problem was to use a felt-tipped pen to write new numbers on the panel above the seats and match this with reservation labels stuck on with tape. This not uncommon challenge meant a total seat reservation labelling process that might not finish until the early hours of the morning. In this situation the only place for me to grab some sleep was on the floor of the small, cupboard-sized stationmaster's office.

But at least this aspect of the preparation could be done without, relatively, real time pressure. In contrast, on the Saturday, customers were soon queuing outside the front of the station behind the heavy wooden destination signs for Newcastle, Birmingham, Bradford and Edinburgh. The incoming trains arrived and disgorged their eager holidaymakers and were then despatched empty to Goodrington sidings. Here they received their turnround clean, such as it was, and had to be equipped with new reservation labels before being brought back into the station Up platform to receive customers from the next queue. In the worst cases the booked turnrounds were only 90 minutes, which put pressure on everyone, and woe betide all concerned if one of the dreaded Western/Midland swaps was also involved.

Once the fully reserved set pulled into the platform, the rush to join the train was far from dignified and was invariably followed by heads appearing at each window complaining of non-existent seats or unauthorised occupation by others. It was at times like this that the need for strict adherence to booked departure times brought the relief of energetic whistle-blowing and flag waving and the comfort of knowing that the problems would gradually be sorted out on the long trip home.

THE SCOTTISH TELEVISION TRAIN

Jim Dorward describes a pioneering Scottish Region example of on-train television broadcasting

It is Wednesday 14 August 1957. The Scottish Region's television train is at Johnstone station on the Glasgow–Ayr line ready for an 8.47 a.m. departure to Oban. It is some twenty years since the first radio reception on trains and today's extraordinary train represents another railway milestone: each coach is equipped with television monitors to display black-and-white television programmes produced and transmitted from the on-board 'studio' housed in

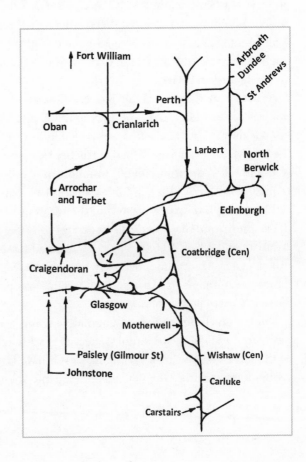

a BG bogie brake van normally used for mail and parcels. Behind the studio vehicle is a Brake Standard Corridor (BSK) coach for the television crew, including an electrician responsible for cabling throughout the train. This is followed by two open coaches with four seats at each table, a buffet car, another two open coaches and finally a coach for the guard. Eight coaches are quite enough for the gradients that will face the two steam engines on the West Highland Line between Craigendoran and Crianlarich Upper.

After picking up more passengers at Elderslie and Paisley (Gilmour Street) the train will proceed to the start of the West Highland Line by travelling through Glasgow between Shields Junction and Bellgrove over a line not used on a regular basis by passenger trains.

Unless they are engrossed in watching the televison programmes, the passengers will notice the train stopping on the single-line West Highland route to cross the all-stations 10 a.m. Arrochar & Tarbet–Craigendoran push-pull train at Garelochhead and the 12.05 p.m. Oban–Glasgow (Buchanan Street) and Edinburgh (Princes Street) at Taynuilt. Arrival at Oban is 1.18 p.m., which will give passengers over 5 hours for sightseeing and shopping. They might even get to see the arrival or departure of the boats serving such places as Tobermory and Barra.

At 6.45 p.m. the train is due to leave Oban and return to Johnstone, but not via the West Highland Line. Instead it will give passengers another scenic line to enjoy, as the train is to travel via Killin Junction and Callander, joining the WCML at Dunblane. When it reaches Glasgow it will use another line (Gushetfaulds Junction–Shields Junction) not used regularly by passenger trains and will arrive back at Johnstone at 11.02 p.m.

This unusual train is busy during the summer season. In July there were departures from Glasgow (Queen Street) to St Andrews, North Berwick, Arbroath and Oban. All four trips could be made on a 50s ticket, saving 9s 7d, not an insignificant sum when only high earners were getting £20 a week. The entertainment on these particular trains was provided by the Glasgow *Evening Citizen* newspaper.

Those travelling on these imaginative trains would probably be torn between watching the beautiful scenery they passed through and the novelty of the scenes on the 'telly'. Some may even have been influenced to spend more money to bring the new technology into their front room.

US RAILROAD STATIONS AND BUILDINGS

———◄○►———

Theo Steel provides a snapshot of a parallel US trend towards the positive reuse of former railway buildings

The background to this piece is a 2009 visit to Roanoke in the US, the spiritual and actual home of the Norfolk and Western Railroad (N&W). We had stayed at the Roanoke Hotel – built in the late nineteenth century and run by the company until 1989 – and had planned to look at a permanent exhibition in the Raymond Loewy-designed art deco station building honouring O. Winston Link, the publisher of a series of evocative 1950s photos of N&W steam.

While it will be a few years (2018 is the schedule) before regular passenger services return to Roanoke, it is also the home of the Virginia Transport Museum where the prize attractions are an N&W J Class locomotive and a Mallet example, along with other exhibits. The works where they were built is also still operating, albeit repairing diesels these days.

At the museum there was a touring exhibition featuring the 150 best buildings in the US, chosen by a consumer panel but, in typical architect's style, much argued and supplemented by their list of ninety-eight that they thought ought to have been there! No less than ten US stations are included.

Grand Central New York, 100 years old in 2013 and beautifully restored, tops the rail list at number thirteen. The others are Washington Union, St Louis, Cincinnati, Los Angeles, Washington Metro, Chicago, Kansas City, Philadelphia 30th Street and a unique entry – the late, lamented Penn station in New York, which was sadly demolished in 1963. They collectively range across US architectural styles from the late nineteenth-century Richardson-esque of St Louis through the Beaux Arts of Grand Central and Kansas City to the art deco of Cincinnati and the Spanish–American art deco of Los Angeles.

The featured stations are mostly large Union stations but it is always worth hunting out other stations in North American towns and cities. Some are still being used for their original purpose while others range from total adaptation (for example, St Louis is now a hotel and shopping centre) through to being busier than ever with train services – Los Angeles is an example with its ninety-plus daily departures these days. Most now combine shopping and restaurant centres with train operations.

A feature of US stations is extensive waiting facilities but often rather drab train-side access, which is sometimes not very appropriate for the volume of customers – the contrast between grand entrance and train access at Grand Central in New York and Washington are cases in point. Other stations like Cincinnati and Kansas City have six trains a week and six a day respectively but are now primarily museum focused. However, after long periods of disuse they have been adapted and are still there.

Some former stations are now shells, such as Buffalo or Detroit, isolated from rail these days and awaiting adaptation. Many have been recently restored. After forty years as a storage warehouse, St Paul Union was given a $247 million refit and reopened as a transportation hub as part of a downtown revival attempt in 2013; Denver and Springfield, Massachusetts are currently awaiting restoration. Many have been pulled down but others have been adapted as banks (Albany, San Antonio) and hotels. Among the hotels are the Chattanooga Choo Choo (complete with sleeping cars to stay in) and Nashville Union.

Adaptation is not limited to large Union stations. The information centre in Eagle River, Wisconsin is the old Chicago N&W railroad station, a number of the New York Central stations along the Hudson Valley have been adapted and the old Baltimore and Ohio (B&O) station at Gaithersburg is a delightful café. Eating gourmet (as well as fast!) food at stations is not impossible. The Oyster Bar in the basement at Grand Central New York is a venerable institution and is now complemented by some modern additions. J.B. Smith's in the old Presidential waiting room at Washington is rather special and Traxx Restaurant at Union station in Los Angeles is fun (currently they only cater for special events), even if it is a pale imitation of the last Harvey House facility designed by Mary Colter. The station at Lake Louise in Canada is a delightful restaurant, with sleepers providing accommodation and courses punctuated by CP freights grinding through.

American-preserved railways are worth visiting for the stations. The Grand Canyon Railway has impressive facilities at both Williams Junction as well as at the rim, where the initial facilities were developed by the Santa Fe Railway. North Conway is straight out of *Dr Zhivago* and the Durango and Silverton facilities have survived remarkably well.

US stations are not renowned for overall roofs and many of those that did exist have been pulled down, such as the one at Boston South. That said, the exhibition centre at Philadelphia is based around Broad Street terminal which features a roof similar to St Pancras but with a larger span.

In Baltimore the B&O Railroad Museum is centred on a set of buildings from the 1840s onwards that are surprisingly intact and you can stay at the B&O headquarters skyscraper dating from 1900, which is now a hotel. The Walters Art Museum in Baltimore was also founded on a railroad fortune. The Sacramento railway heritage goes back to the 1860s and Pullman, the railway town in the Chicago suburbs, is surprisingly well preserved.

US railroad magnates of the nineteenth century did not skimp on their private housing – The Frick Collection art museum in New York is perhaps the most famous example, once home to industrialist Henry Clay Frick, but there is also Flagler's mansion in Palm Beach and various Vanderbilt houses. A personal favourite is the James Hill house in St Paul. Their private vehicles were often very luxurious too and over 200 are still operating to brighten up an Amtrak station or train.

This is just a snapshot to whet appetites, but most of the stations can be found on the Internet and there are many books on the subject. I find it encouraging that, as in the UK, we have moved from destruction to preservation and that the US financial structures have encouraged so much reuse and adaptation to move us forward from the 'Amshacks' of the 1970s.

NEW STATIONMASTER

———◦———

Fernley Maker's first appointment as a stationmaster was typical of the railway in the 1950s

I was appointed to the post of stationmaster/goods agent at Northfield in 1952 but had to wait until the following April to be released from my post as passenger clerk at Bude. Northfield lay on the old Midland Railway Main Line from Birmingham–Bristol, some 7½ miles south of Birmingham New Street. The main station building was located on an island platform between the Up and Down main lines with Up and Down goods lines beyond, the latter normally worked on the permissive block system. In every 24 hours there were some 200 train movements, including calls by forty-two passenger services. The fifty-five-lever signal box was situated at the south end of the station and the goods yard consisted of three thirty-wagon sidings, a crane siding, goods office, weighbridge, feedstuffs stores and a garage for the railway motor vehicle.

I was fortunate in getting good 'digs' while waiting for the stationmaster's house to become available. This was situated at the entrance to the goods yard and of typical Midland Railway design: two reception rooms, three bedrooms, a kitchen with just a cold-water tap, an outside lavatory and a large garden. Rent and rates were 12s 6d a week, which went up when a small pantry was subsequently converted into a bathroom.

My induction into the new post was brief and cursory. The relief stationmaster went home as soon as I arrived on the Monday but was back with me for Tuesday and Wednesday. That was it. His return on the Saturday allowed me to get back to Bude for the weekend but from the following Monday it was all down to me.

Halesowen Junction signal box, about 1½ miles south of Northfield, was also under my supervision. It too was a busy place, with four running lines plus the branch to Longbridge motor works and on to Halesowen. This was worked under electric-train staff regulations with ex-London & North Western permissive instruments in the box contrasting with the usual three-position needle instruments for the absolute block on the main lines. Father and son Jack and Maurice Roberts both worked the box, the former a devout member of the Plymouth Brethren and someone who encouraged me to work the frame for experience during the period I was in lodgings. In the busy period between 6 p.m. and 8 p.m. pulling levers along the seventy-five-lever frame and dealing with the clamouring bells of the block instruments was truly hard graft.

One of my Northfield signalmen was Bill Taylor, who had started out as a van boy at Birmingham's Lawley Street depot but had been at Northfield for many years. He made sure I could work the box there. I also remember him because in a quiet period of about 20 minutes just after 9 a.m. each day he would have a full fry-up in the box, something that produced a mouth-watering aroma and smelled especially tantalising to one who had managed only toast for his breakfast quite a bit earlier. Someone else who helped me a lot with operating matters at this time was Raymond George who was the district signalling inspector for the Birmingham Midland area and one of the best practical railwaymen I ever met.

I was fortunate with my staff at Northfield. Former army captain A.B. Pettit was my goods clerk, a church lay reader and well respected by our traders. With the help of our checker and motor vehicle driver the yard dealt with a variety of full-load business, coal, animal feeding stuffs, containers and steel for new flats springing up in the area. In addition there was a large quantity of returned empties, both forwarded and received and always difficult and time-consuming to identify and handle. Access to the yard was off the Up goods line via points released from the signal box and operated for shunting purposes by the platform porter. Our inwards 'pick-up' freight service detached wagons around 9.15 a.m. and returned to shunt the yard about 12.30 p.m.

Northfield was a very good starting place for a new stationmaster, with plenty of variety in the work from the daily routine to occasional signal and engine failures and acting as pilotman for SLW. Less dramatic was the collection of small accounts locally and inspections of damaged goods in connection with the claims procedures.

Not everything went smoothly, of course. One of the porters booked on at midnight to attend to an excursion train arrived to find the booking office had been burgled. Needing to call me out, he was so nervous that the burglars might still be around that he insisted the signalman accompany him and then waited until I had dressed in order to have support on the way back to the office. And then there was a relief goods checker called Harry who spent his lunchtime in the local pub and seemed seriously short of energy when he returned in the afternoon. On one occasion when there were two 10-ton wagons of Bibbys animal-feeding stuffs to unload and Harry was making little progress with the job, I took the late-turn platform porter with me to the yard and roused Harry from his lethargy.

The porter and I unloaded from the wagons and had Harry running with the sack barrow until he was sweating profusely – we had cleared the first wagon and Harry had got the message about tackling the other one.

I had only been at Northfield for eight months when, due to a shortage of relief staff, I was requested to undertake the stationmaster duties for King's Norton, the next station, and to cover my own position as overtime. The King's Norton post was a much higher graded one, the location having a shunting yard and carriage-cleaning staff. This was deep-end treatment but I managed to survive for a five-week period and benefitted from the extra

In Cotswold country, 4-6-0 No. 4086 *Builth Castle* heads through Campden with the 2 p.m. Worcester–Paddington service.

money. I also covered Barnt Green and Bournville for odd days and, coming back off leave on one occasion, I found I had to cover King's Heath for a week, a station I had never even seen before.

The organisational set-up in the Birmingham area was complicated. Operationally there were two district operating superintendents at New Street, as the Western and Midland Division had separate control and general offices but shared a staff office. Commercial responsibility was bi-regional with a district passenger manager at New Street and a district goods manager at Snow Hill, where the Western Region's district operating superintendent was also based. One of the consequences was a lot of meetings involving us stationmasters.

On a less functional note, one of my enduring memories of Northfield is being in the garden on a summer evening at about 9.30 p.m., just as the light was beginning to fade. Rushing through the station at about 70mph would come the Up mail, hauled by a usually spotless LMS Jubilee-Class locomotive with about seven passenger coaches and two TPO mail coaches behind. About 10 minutes later the Down mail, similarly formed, could be heard in the distance, soon coming into sight with the Jubilee pulling against the uphill grade, the TPOs and tail lamp disappearing into the twilight and the Down main signal dropping to the horizontal behind it. There were also Up and Down mail trains in the early hours but I seldom saw them, although I think they may have registered subconsciously while I was in the Land of Nod.

ON FROM NORTHFIELD

————◆◇▸————

After five years as stationmaster/goods agent at Northfield,
Fernley Maker was ready to move on

On 1 August 1957 I reported to the offices of the district operating superintendent (Midland) at Gloucester Eastgate seeking appointment to a Class 3 post as a relief stationmaster. The grade was the same as that at Northfield but overtime, expenses and Sunday working would make the earnings appreciably higher and I would be nearer to Cornwall where my wife was temporarily living.

My first interview with the chief staff clerk, W.J. Wilcox, did not go well. I had crossed swords with 'Brummagem Bill', as he was known, when I was at Northfield and his long list of detailed questions gave me a strong feeling he did not want me to get the job. I then saw District Operating Superintendent C.W. Hearnshaw and received a totally different reception. He promised a few days refreshing before taking me for my rules and regulations competence.

All went well. I got the job and, with the help of the Cheltenham stationmaster, found lodgings, passed my rules grilling and went to my first relief job at Bredon. I subsequently found a furnished flat so that my wife could join me and a few months later we moved into a brand-new house near Lansdown station. Before that happened I had found that my chief staff clerk nemesis was reluctant to issue passes for my weekend visits home. On one occasion he actually sent me to Towcester for two weeks with the comment, 'You will not be able to get home from there.' Fortunately the office clerks were more sympathetic and tried to help without 'Brummagem Bill' knowing.

The Gloucester district covered an interesting area, extending from the Lickey Incline and Abbotswood Junction to Bristol St Philips and Bath with branches to Upton-on-Severn, Stroud, Dursley and Sharpness – also the route from Ashchurch via Broom Junction and all the way east to Stratford-upon-Avon and Towcester. During my first months I covered most of the stations in the district and the yardmaster's posts at Gloucester Upper yard, Westerleigh and Bristol St Philips. The junior relief stationmasters also had to cover the posts of stationmaster's clerk at Gloucester and Cheltenham.

It was a time of continuing reorganisation and Gloucester finished up with a larger district bounded by Blackwell, Moreton-in-Marsh, Stow-on-the-Wold, Purton, Berkeley Road, Awre Junction, Fawley and Stoke Edith. I was kept pretty busy and in one particular week I covered the stationmaster's clerk position at Eastgate during the day and then worked in Lansdown booking office until 10 p.m. On the Saturday I did the half-day at Gloucester and the whole of the late turn at Cheltenham, following it up with a Sunday turn as well. With a new house and mortgage the money was useful, and the work more congenial than the occasion when I had to go from Upton-on-Severn to Lansdown and take over from staff suspected of serious irregularities.

During my five years in the job I worked at nearly every possible location in the district and undertook a host of special tasks. The latter included assisting at Standish Junction on Saturdays during the holiday season, the box there controlling both the Bristol and Stroud lines and having a very busy time with trains on the Midland line and on the GWR route via Honeybourne, as well as the Swindon–Gloucester locals. One of the few stations I had not relieved at was Moreton-in-Marsh and strangely, or as a bit of staff office enterprise, I found myself sent there for two weeks before being appointed to the permanent stationmaster/goods agent position.

Located in the lovely North Cotswolds, Moreton was a rather 'feudal' station, with a well-regulated existence and staff who had been there for ages and were quite set in their ways. It served a wealthy area and gave us many first-class passengers with very regular travel habits and who were the prey of station foreman Harry, who had an unerring sense of who would produce the best tip. Goods clerk Wesley who stepped in to cover the daily gap between the early and late booking office turns was another character. He invariably wore a long raincoat and a trilby hat that was turning green with age and kept his cycle clips on all day. He sang in the church choir and apparently even kept the clips on beneath his cassock. Even train crews seemed to have their unusual habits, with those detained for any length of time in our Down goods loop apparently having temporary membership of the nearby British Legion Club.

After a couple of years my tenure at Moreton was cut short by more reorganisation which made me redundant and, in 1966, saw me covering the post of area manager at Evesham where one incident in particular sticks in my memory. It followed the reporting of a broken rail in the long section between Evesham and Pershore. The only available spare rail was in Evesham yard and, as luck would have it, there was a diesel locomotive on hand as well. Unfortunately there were no ordinary wagons on which to load the rail, just a small ex-GWR special shunters truck – hardly an ideal vehicle for the task.

After some local consultation with the permanent-way staff we contrived to get the rail on to the shunters truck, securely lashed down but with an overhang of some 8ft at the rear and almost sagging to the ballast. A red flag was tied to the end of the rail, the permanent-way gang jumped on and off we went, albeit slowly and not without some anxiety. We had just over an hour before the next train was due and no time was lost in the process of unloading, cutting and replacing. Returning hastily, and certainly a lot faster than when we set out, we just managed to get our train put 'inside' at Pershore with not more than a very small delay to the following train.

THE LOCO

———<o>———

As part of his TA training, Geoff Body spent five weeks
at the busy and varied March motive power depot

Located between March station and Whitemoor marshalling yard, March 'Loco' was an important activity centre with all the facilities needed to look after its 143 locomotives, as well as the lesser needs of the many others which arrived on inwards services and required the normal turnround facilities before taking up their return working.

It was a busy area altogether in railway terms, and one with very varied motive power requirements. March station itself dealt with passenger trains on the East Anglia–Doncaster/York route via the Great Northern and Great Eastern Joint Line, along with those via Ely to and from Peterborough and beyond and the numerous local services including those on the Wisbech/

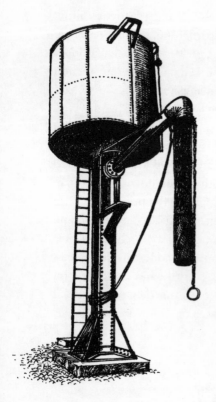

Water cranes like this were an essential and common feature in the days of steam. (Roy Gallop)

King's Lynn and St Ives branches. Freight activities centred around Whitemoor, which had a constant stream of trains feeding the voracious capacity of its Up hump. Re-sorted, their loads moved on to London and East Anglia, with a balancing movement of empties and evening express departures from the Down side of the complex.

March depot's own locomotive fleet was very varied with V2 2-6-2 (six engines) and B17 4-6-0 (twelve engines) classes for the prestige passenger services, D16 4-4-0s (six) for local passenger trains, K1 and K3 2-6-0s (twenty-five and nineteen respectively) for coal trains and empties, O1 and WD big freight machines (twenty-five and fifteen) and a host of various J Class 0-6-0s (thirty-four) for the mixed-traffic role they filled everywhere. There was one 9F-Class engine and ten diesel electrics.

The March engines were maintained in the main shed between their dates for 'shopping', with the major overhaul usually carried out where the locomotive had been built. This interval was based on time and mileage considerations to ensure that there would be no failure in traffic.

Incoming 'foreign' power (i.e. engines from other depots diagrammed to carry out another job after attention) required different facilities. Their needs would be met by March's coaling plant, turntable, sand supply, ashpit and water crane. March also had an inspection tunnel to allow checking for steam leaks and a shed for boiler washing out.

The March depot footplate staff were organised into fifteen 'links'. Drivers started in the Junior Spare Link and progressed to Link 9, which manned the express passenger services, after which responsibility would lessen by moving to the local passenger and goods links and then to purely local jobs in the pre-retirement years. The task of managing men and machines at a large depot like March was highly complex and depended heavily on the mechanical and running foremen and on the outside foremen controlling the ashpit area, the three-hopper coaling plant and the movements to and from the electric turntable.

My footplate week came as a pleasant change from crawling into a firebox, building a brick arch and trying to distinguish a cracked stay by tapping the candidates with a hammer. The first day saw me allocated to Diagram 17 and booking on to join Driver Wakeling and Fireman Burgess on Class B17 2-6-0 locomotive No. 61643 *Champion Lodge*. We dropped down to March station to take over the Newcastle–Lowestoft passenger train, getting away at 2.03 p.m. and arriving at Thorpe station in Norwich at 3.56 p.m. Released to the locomotive depot beside the passenger station, the tasks of coaling, taking water and turning on the turntable left us plenty of time to eat our 'snap' before leaving the loco at 7.18 p.m. to head up the 7.38 p.m. Class D partially fitted freight service to Whitemoor. There were no problems but the journey back over the same route took twice as long and it was 10.19 p.m. before we got back, and we still had to get from the yard reception road to the loco depot.

Diagram 19 the next day meant booking on at 9.54 a.m. in readiness for hauling a Parkeston Quay–Liverpool service between March and Sheffield and then heading the same service back again. With Driver Ward and Fireman Ellington we had again been allocated a B17 2-6-0, this time No. 61619 *Welbeck Abbey*, but it was to prove a much tougher trip than the one to Norwich and back. For a start 61619 was fresh out of shops and, despite a bit of running in, was very 'stiff in the bushes'. Any locomotive wheel arrangement that results in a driving wheel beneath the cab produces more movement on the footplate than occurs with 4-6-2 and 2-6-2 wheel arrangements, and the combination of the two factors meant a lot of oscillation on the *Welbeck Abbey* footplate and a need to watch out for the sawing motion of the plate covering the join with the tender.

Our journey from leaving March at 10.34 a.m. to arriving at Sheffield at 1.11 p.m. with a heavy load was a struggle all the way. This bad day did not improve on the return either for, unrefreshed through having had to attend to our own engine, we took over a late runner and simply could not overcome the delay, though not for want of trying. It was a hard trip, interesting and also memorable for my first experience of running through a tunnel, with the bright glow from the open firebox door reflecting on the speeding walls enclosing us and turning the noise of our passage into an eerie scene of demonic symphony. Arrival back at March after nearly another 3 hours of struggle proved something of a relief.

Apart from one hiccup, my third footplate day was excellent. I was with Driver Head and Fireman Robinson when they booked on at 9.34 a.m. and took V2 Class 2-6-2 No. 60803 out to work the 9.54 a.m. departure from March (the Lowestoft–Newcastle train) as far as York. I knew these V2s to be special in terms of power and reliability and quite capable of taking on pretty well any job within their route availability. I now found out what easy riding they offered, something that made all the difference to my spell of firing. Not only could I keep my feet and get the shovel to the firebox door without mishap, but I could begin to position the coal where it was most needed, that is, where the fire burned brightest. My companions were good company and busied themselves with regulator, notching up and injectors so that I would not feel watched.

The one bad moment came at Retford. I had dropped down on to the platform to stretch my legs for a moment and when Driver Head asked, 'OK, mate?' I thoughtlessly took it as an enquiry as to my wellbeing and was rather shaken when he took my 'Yes' as me having seen the guard's 'right away' signal and accordingly opened the regulator. Fortunately, no passenger was half in and half out of the train but there could have been a bad outcome.

I had recovered my equanimity by the time we got to York and there was no time there to brood over what might have been as we had only an hour before taking over the 2.50 p.m. return working. Our hurried meal in the mess room was enlivened for me by trying to gauge just how much my Norfolk driver and a Geordie he was talking to – both in full dialect – could understand one another. Back into March at 6.27 p.m. after another good run, I felt much better than when I had parted with *Welbeck Abbey* the previous evening.

My two remaining footplate days proved somewhat less glamorous, both involving out and home freight trains. On the Thursday I booked on at 7.55 a.m. for Diagram 313, to which Class O1 2-8-0 No. 63875 had been allocated, along with Driver Bradman and Fireman Southwell. We had half an hour in which to leave the depot and get back on to the Class F unbraked train of coal empties in the Down departure sidings and then just 2 hours to get it to Pyewipe yard, just north of Lincoln.

Our diagram had a layover of nearly 3 hours but then we had what seemed like a bit of luck: we were to leave earlier and bring back a Class C special fast freight. After a mad scramble to collect tools from the stores we climbed on to Class K3 2-6-0 No. 61887 and set about bringing the fire up to scratch. We soon discovered that not only was 61887 a bad riding and noisy engine but the injector was wasting water badly and she just did not steam well. Still, with a great deal of clanking from the motion, we kept going and limped into Whitemoor at 3.30 p.m. after an anxious trip.

There was more injector trouble on my Friday outward engine, a Class B1 4-6-0 No. 61360, but nothing very serious. Working Diagram 249, Driver Bird and Fireman Lacey had her prepared and got her round to the Up departure sidings in good time to leave Whitemoor at 10.40 a.m. on a Class H goods trip to Bury St Edmunds. Despite a hot big end, our B1 did not have a heavy load and completed the outward journey via Newmarket without loss of time. The mess room at Bury was a poor place and we were quite glad to see the back of it and take over another B1, No. 61252, for the return journey. With a Class D goods and clear signals we covered the distance in 40 minutes less than on the morning run, pulling into Whitemoor reception roads at 3.25 p.m.

Later on I was to have training periods at Norwich diesel depot and at Ilford electric traction depot, both highly instructive but not quite as exciting as the time spent amid the grime and constant activity at March Loco.

THE GREAT EAST MIDLANDS STORM

———◦———

Chris Blackman had to resort twice to some impromptu saw work to rectify storm damage

One afternoon in January 1976 when I was assistant area manager at Leicester, the East Midlands was hit by a tremendous storm. I had barely got home, and certainly not drunk my tea, when Nottingham Control rang to advise me that an automatic half-barrier on the Leicester–Melton Mowbray line had failed and there were reports that a train had passed over the crossing before the barriers had come down. This was not good news, with a strong suggestion of a 'wrong side failure'. Within 2 minutes the tea was in a Thermos flask, my box of emergency equipment had been loaded into the van and I was on my way, dodging odd bits of tree debris in the road.

As I arrived at the crossing I carried out a quick inspection and noted that all the red zig-zag lights were fully working but one of the barriers had become entangled with a tree that had partially blown down. I discussed the situation with the signalman and took local control of the crossing, then advised the police that their presence was no longer necessary.

At this point the owner of the house nearest the crossing emerged to find out was going on and why the police blue light was flashing. When I explained the position Mr Neighbour became Mr Helpful and said he would go and get his chainsaw. Five minutes later he was back and we set to work to free the tree from the barrier, a task that was achieved without any damage apparent to the barrier. By this time the technicians had arrived and tested the equipment. After witnessing the correct operation of the barriers when the next train passed, I advised Control and we all went home, but not before I had thanked Mr Helpful for his assistance and promised him and his wife a complimentary return ticket to London or Skegness. Mr Helpful, now Mr Grateful, duly toddled off home with his handy chainsaw!

I drove home from the barrier-crossing location, negotiating yet more fallen branches and wondering what else the night might have in store. Sure enough, 5 minutes after I reached the house, Control rang to say that all communication had been lost between Syston North and Sileby signal boxes on the main line north of Leicester. I set out again and on arrival at Syston I watched a parcels train coming to a stand at the Up main home signal, having passed slowly through the section under the time interval procedure to examine the line. The driver reported that the Up main was clear but the Down and Up goods line had an obstruction of some sort about half a mile back towards Sileby.

Frank Granger, the permanent-way inspector, arrived at this moment and together we set out along the Up goods to investigate the obstruction. We struggled forward leaning at about 45 degrees into the wind! Eventually our Bardic lamps revealed a dark mass across the goods lines, which turned out to be the roof of a very large garden shed. It was far too heavy to lift, and I was just wondering what we should do next when, like some magic trick, Frank produced a large saw – from where I know not, as it was far too big to fit into a knapsack or a coat pocket, but then Frank was one of a remarkable breed called p-way inspectors.

Twenty minutes later we had sawn the shed roof into reasonably sized chunks and then it was just a matter of saying 'one, two, three, heave' into the air and letting the wind simply take the chunks clear of the lineside fencing into the adjacent field for the farmer to puzzle over the next day.

SCIENTIFIC SERVICES

———◇———

As Brian Arbon discovered, some people get set in their ways and are unwilling to listen to younger folk

In this book and its predecessors there are numerous references to the traffic apprenticeship scheme, which recruited graduates and staff members in roughly equal numbers for special training. By 1960, the year I joined, the three-year programme was made up of two years 'sitting with Nellie' and one year of supernumerary jobs. It had, seemingly, run unchanged for a number of years and was in need of an overhaul. Indeed, graduates were beginning to resign part-way through the training, which I suspect was pretty well unheard of previously. In my experience it tended to be pot luck how you got on with the people you were assigned to. Most were informative and friendly and went out of their way to involve you in anything out of the ordinary, but there were a resentful few who were barely communicative.

There was one such at the small station where, after a short induction course at Derby, my training experience began. One of the lectures at Derby was about the new research department near Alexandra Palace that must have been recently centralised from various regional establishments. Anyway, after a week or two at my small station, the fearsome female keeper from the nearby resident crossing stormed in with what looked like a glass pickled-onion jar full of cloudy, brown water, complaining vociferously that the well (her source of drinking water) was contaminated.

The chief (and only full-time) clerk told her he would send it to the laboratory at Doncaster for analysis, as he had evidently done before. I somewhat timidly suggested that it should be addressed to 'Alexandra Palace', but what could I possibly know, a railwayman of just one month against his forty odd years, so off went the glass jar of dirty water with its tied-on brown label on the train en route to Doncaster.

About a fortnight later a stranger alighted on the platform from the train and came into the office. He introduced himself as from 'Scientific Services at Alexandra Palace' and produced from his briefcase the jagged glass neck of our pickle jar, complete with lid and label. 'This was forwarded to us from Doncaster,' he said. 'Can you tell me what this once contained?'

FILMING GAFFER

—◁◦▷—

Chris Blackman was twice a reluctant film-making aide and both times his reluctance proved well founded

The Willesden-area movements inspector's duties covered all safety concerning line matters, attending emergencies and mishaps, visiting signal boxes and other locations and biennial examinations of signalmen and other grades. Additionally, investigation of train delays and irregularities, SLW and weekend engineering work were all part of the regular routine. I was never bored! The last line of the official list of my duties was 'other duties as directed', a wonderful catch-all as far as management was concerned.

Eric Ball, the area manager, sent for me one day to 'direct' one of those 'other duties'.

'We've got a film company who want to come and do some filming on a railway location,' he said. 'I've agreed that they can use South West sidings as there is no other activity in there during the daytime. Just keep an eye on them, make sure the sidings are secured, and that they don't do anything silly. Oh, and by the way, Chris, I remember doing a few of these filming larks in the days when I was a DI – you can be sure of getting a nice fat tip. Good luck.' With that he gave me the details and an instruction to ring the company straightaway.

The following week, as arranged, I turned out at 8.30 a.m., ensured that the sidings were secured out of use and an appropriate entry made and signed in the signal box before walking over to meet the film crew at the street entrance to South West sidings. Their plan was to film the pop star P.J. Proby singing one of his ditties whilst strolling along the sidings. I never bothered to ask them why!

The crew assembled all their kit, the make-up girls laid out their stuff on a table by the buffer stops, and we awaited the arrival of the star who rolled up in a limousine looking as though he had just got out of bed. While the make-up girls fussed around, the crew tried to lay out their little tramway for the camera. It wouldn't fit properly along the siding track, so I sprang into action, having decided to be supremely helpful and to justify the handsome tip that Eric Ball had said was sure to come my way.

'If you like I could arrange to get a platelayers' trolley for the cameraman,' I said. They agreed this would be more than welcome. I trotted off to fetch such a trolley, assembled it with assistance from the local p-way ganger at the top end of the sidings and pushed it gently down towards the buffer stops where Proby was still being attended to by gushing make-up girls. The camera crew were delighted. 'Joe' was deputed to push it and naturally I said I would help him, particularly as I would have to be responsible for stopping it in an emergency – well, at least chucking a sprag into the wheel.

By now it was mid morning and the summer sun was shining brightly. I removed my jacket, bottles of water were distributed to the crew and I was left in the dry!

Then the filming commenced. Music sounded – Proby's latest hit, apparently – and the audio technicians announced they were satisfied everything was working OK. Proby took up position in front of the buffer stop and the cameraman fixed his camera on the trolley and climbed aboard. At the command 'Take 1', Joe and I started to push towards the other end of the siding and Proby's latest hit could be heard all the way to Wormwood Scrubs. Remarkable voice I thought, before I realised that it was purely a recording and the great P.J. Proby himself, ambling along some 10yd behind me, was simply miming. After adjustments and several takes, the crew broke for their lunch and I dived out to the chippy; the sun by now was even hotter than the chips.

After lunch there were some more takes and Joe found a deputy, but I was left to sweat it out in the heat until the director announced he was satisfied. Proby went off in his limousine, the crew jumped in their van and I was left penniless to return the trolley and stow it next to the platelayers' cabin.

Eric Ball thought the conclusion was hilarious. When he sent for me the following week he could scarcely keep a straight face. 'We've had a message from that film company to say that they would like to do another day's filming next Wednesday as the camera wasn't working properly, and all the film has been lost.'

I remembered I had something else scheduled for Wednesday ...

Some time later I was summoned to see Eric Ball for further direction. This time a different film company wanted to film scenes in a railway carriage the following Tuesday. Before I could utter a word Eric added that he had already checked to see that I had no other duties scheduled that day. I accepted with good grace that I had been outmanoeuvred! Eric handed me the papers and said that he had instructed Stonebridge Park Maintenance Depot to clean and prepare three coaches for the day.

When I turned up on the Tuesday, Stonebridge had done a splendid job on the three coaches placed at the buffer stops end of the siding and had clipped and scotched the entrance points to prevent any movement towards the vehicles. The coaches were a Tourist Standard Open (TSO) (sixty-four-seat second-class open), an FK (first-class corridor coach) and a BSK. Excellent, I thought, they will have the choice of first or second class and compartment or open saloon stock.

I met the crew, who turned out to be from an Italian film company. With the help of their interpreter I gave them a safety briefing, assisted them as they

In his relief signalman days, Chris Blackman discusses a train-regulating issue in the Willesden power signal box. (Chris Blackman)

climbed up into the BSK, walked them through the train and then enquired where they wished to start. They looked aghast! There were mutterings to the interpreter – were there other coaches they could use? I explained that we had prepared coaches with a variety of layouts and classes from which they could choose something suitable. More mutterings, but much louder and with some irritation – clearly the coaches were not suitable.

What did they want? As a musician I have a little knowledge of Italian, but limited to what is found in music scores. It doesn't include detailed descriptions of railway carriages and their suitability or otherwise. Fortunately the interpreter then called for silence and explained, with much gesticulating, what was wanted. This differed markedly from the brief I had been given. The company wished to shoot a scene from pre-war Italy involving three gangsters; well, three at the beginning of the scene and two at the end. To shoot(!) this scene in a convincing way meant having a vehicle that could pass muster as a 1930s Italian railway coach; in other words, ancient and grubby!

Further gesticulations pointed me to a vehicle on the stop blocks of the adjacent siding – an old mess coach with 'Condemned' painted on the side. This, they said, was just what they wanted. Clearly Stonebridge Park's efforts were going to be wasted and I mused that whilst Mussolini may have made the trains run to time he had obviously made no impact on cleanliness of rolling stock. So we adjourned to the mess coach. After a couple of hours they had done enough takes – quickly achieved with much loud shouting in Italian and occasional gunshots from the sound-effects man, accompanied by liberal spraying of tomato ketchup. By lunchtime they were finished – presumably the afternoon would be devoted to a siesta – and after much handshaking and smiles all round they left, but not before the director's sidekick had thanked me profusely in broken English and pressed a bundle of notes into my hand. I escorted them to the gate, went back to clear up but decided that the ketchup merged satisfactorily with the other detritus left by years of mess from weekend engineering work.

On the train back to Willesden, tired but with a sense of anticipation, I reached into my pocket to fish out and count the bundle of notes for half a day's 'work as directed'. It consisted entirely of Italian lira!

I didn't tell Eric Ball.

QUICK THINKERS AND SLOW THINKERS

Ian Body described the different reactions of two Worcester area signalmen

Relief signalmen have always been a breed apart; able to work a wide variety of signal boxes and willing to accommodate highly irregular rosters, even to the point of sometimes being paid for travelling back from one shift while in fact already having started their next one. But, like any group of people, they varied in speed of thought, as two examples demonstrate.

In the first it was a Thursday night at Worcester Tunnel Junction signal box which, at the time, was one end of a midweek engineering possession, the other being further north at Droitwich. I was the pilotman and was waiting to accompany the next northbound service while the detonator protection was being undertaken by a dependable relief signalman – although not one normally known for his exertion.

At this stage the engineer had dug a sizable hole in the Up line running towards Worcester, so when we received an unexpected two bells for 'Train Entering Section' from Droitwich at the pilotman end our laidback relief signalman did two things. Firstly he looked at me to see if my face was suggesting I was thinking what he was thinking and then he leapt up, burst out of the door, flew down the steps and fled northwards through the tunnel to put detonators down and frantically wave a red light to stop the southbound freight service heading towards a hole certainly large enough to derail it. He achieved this aim, we propelled the service back towards Droitwich and he spent the rest of the turn in the signal-box chair. And I don't recall him breaking into a trot ever again.

At the opposite end of the scale, I had cause to carry out a signal-box visit to Norton Junction where the line south to Bristol branches off the Worcester–Evesham–Oxford route. As I reached the top of the steps I could clearly hear the radio covering a cricket test match (it was understood by all that radios were not permitted in signal boxes, as it was seen as a distraction).

As I entered I saw that the relief signalman, an esteemed member of the trade union's Sectional Council, had thrown his copy of the *Daily Express* over the radio in a decidedly slow-thinking solution to this perceived misdemeanour. What followed was a box inspection, a cup of tea and some discussion of differing opinions on union matters, all with the background noise of the test match and the pretence of there being nothing under the newspaper. While it seemed of dubious value to make a major issue of the matter at the time, a pointed stare made my attitude clear and this proved something that did lend the management 'side' some degree of leverage at future union meetings for a while.

YESTERDAY'S TOOLS, YESTERDAY'S SKILLS

A chance remark led Bryan Stone to reflect on former railway practices and equipment

In 1969 I was ordered by BR to go to Switzerland where I would spend twenty-five years developing container-freight traffic in company with railwaymen and women from all over Europe. So it was that when Roger Kreutz, a big, practical SNCF operations man from Strasbourg, came back from a meeting in Derby in about 1971 he sought me out.

'Bryan,' he said, 'I couldn't believe it; there were goods trains coupled only with chains and with no brakes.' Yes it was so. Today I wonder just what we were doing.

Let's start with the standard goods wagons; four-wheeled vehicles on a 10ft wheelbase with spindle buffers and a three-link coupling on the drawbar hook. There were flatbed, five and six-plank, metal-body and enclosed van varieties, all braked, not from the engine but by brake blocks actuated from a side lever applied by hand. Steep gradients would have a notice requiring these brakes on the wagons of a loose-coupled goods train to be pinned down by pulling down the lever and inserting a pin through a rack to hold the brakes on. The process would then have to be reversed at the foot of the incline.

Pinning down brakes often had to be done on the move when shunting. This involved running alongside the wagon and wedging the brake stick (a stout wooden baton about 3ft long) between the brake lever and the wagon spring and pinning it in position. Riding on the brake stick was forbidden, but often done.

Coal and similar bulk commodities were transported in loose-coupled trains whose wagons had what Roger had called 'chains' linking them. These were more properly three-link couplings with one end flattened so as to fit snugly on the wagon coupling hook. To couple up, a shunting pole was used to drop the outer link over the coupling hook of the adjacent wagon. Experienced guards and shunters could do wonders with these stout, wooden poles about 2in thick and 7ft long. At the end was a metal hook with a slight twist.

The actual coupling-up involved hooking the shunting pole into the end link of the coupling hanging from a stationary wagon and, as the next wagon

At Colwick yard one shunter brakes wagons heads into the sorting sidings while two others wait to do the same. (Bryan Stone)

approached, swinging the coupling up so that it dropped on to the hook on the moving one. The coupling was too heavy to lift, so swinging was needed with a well-timed twist to extricate the shunting pole. A miss meant the standing wagon moved away under the impact and having to ask the driver to close up again.

Uncoupling was easier but also needed precise timing. You would rest your pole on the buffer casting – not the shank or the pole would get crunched as the buffer compressed – with the hook beneath the end of the coupling. Then, as the engine pushed and the coupling went slack, a tug on the pole's outer end levered the coupling up and freed it to drop away. This meant that the uncoupled wagon was free to roll, which could be what you wanted if the points were set and the destination siding was clear. The handbrake could then be pinned down to hold it in place. If you forgot, and sometimes one did for there was a lot to think about, a wagon might set off on its own, bent on impact or finishing up in quite the wrong place.

Three link couplings had a lot of slack, with up to 3ft difference between taut couplings and the compressed buffers of closed-up wagons. On a sixty-wagon mineral train the total slack could amount to 180ft, and two people were acutely aware of this. One was the driver, who felt the slack taken up on starting and disappearing as wagons 'buffered up' on braking. The second was the guard, who also took careful notice of the slack, for as the locomotive gathered speed and its load gathered progressive impetus the guard's van could be jerked into motion quite violently. Its occupant learned to listen to the slack being taken up and to brace himself!

There were many variations on this theme, including using the downhill energy of a train to help with the following climb and alleviating the consequences of a broken coupling, something that could easily result from 'snatching'. In his 20-ton, four-wheel brake van the guard's handbrake could not only help if a stop was required, or to hold a train in position, but it could be used to keep the couplings taut if the guard 'knew the road' and when to use it. It required great skill to work a loose-coupled train safely and cleanly.

Many wagons were in poor condition at this time. Even in the early 1960s some still had wooden frames and all were fearfully badly treated. By this time grease boxes were history, but oil axle boxes and journals were not above reproach. Trains were examined at stipulated places and the sound of the wheel-tapper's hammer was a familiar one. He did much more, of course, especially with springs and running gear, dragging brakes and so on, and also minor repairs. Wagons could lose buffers, spring bolts or door fastenings, but most destructive were dry bearings. When the oil was low, a wagon would not get far before the bearing overheated and the 'white metal' surface melted. Soon the last oil would burn and the journal end in the bearing would get red hot, leaving a pungent trail of smoke and making an angry howl. If it was not spotted, a broken axle was highly possible and a derailment inevitable. Closing signal boxes at night in districts where stations were few, combined with old oil-box wagons and higher speeds, meant that hot boxes became a serious problem on some cross-country routes.

Not all trains were loose coupled. Increasingly there were fitted freights, with vacuum brake throughout their length, enabling the driver to run faster and brake the train like a passenger train. A train divided as a result of a broken coupling meant that both parts came to a stop as the vacuum that held the brakes off was destroyed. Another variant was a partly fitted freight train – one with a 'fitted head' of vacuum-braked wagons behind the engine and the rest running unbraked and loose coupled.

One such train, an Up goods with a fitted head, was involved in a major freight-train pile up at Wood Green in June 1963. The rear end of the train was unusually heavy with several bogie-bolster wagons loaded with steel piles and some loaded steel hopper wagons, and these did not stop when the diesel engine D1509 did. Empty 6-ton, flat container wagons had been used to separate the steel-carrying bogie bolsters and cater for any overhang, one of which succumbed to the laws of physics and collapsed under the unsustainable pressure. The steel piles took off and became battering rams as they spread out on the adjoining platform of the station. Mercifully it was empty, but had one of the old wooden Quad-Art suburban coaches sets been there it would have been a disaster. As it was, the clearing up took two whole days.

To couple vacuum-braked wagons meant getting underneath to lift a heavy and dirty screw coupling and ensure the two vacuum pipes engaged properly. Even then there were often difficulties in maintaining the required vacuum pressure, but the dividends of more brakes acting on more wheels were high. One benefit was that some four-wheeled vehicles, lettered XP and carrying special traffics like fish, meat and livestock, could be attached to passenger trains. Valuable horses often travelled this way but such vehicles were not really meant for higher speeds and also required special arrangements to attach, detach and shunt them.

At my first station, Sawbridgeworth, there was a sharply curved siding into the maltings. Two-axle vans could go in and out, but no locomotives so a

In this 1963 mishap at Wood Green the sheer weight of the heavy steel load has overwhelmed the 6-ton Conflat wagon that is used to deal with the overhang. (Bryan Stone)

fine, old draft horse did the work, although sadly it was replaced by a small mechanical tractor before I got my camera into action. The railway-horse culture finally ended, fittingly at Newmarket, but is yet another example of the trades that existed within the period railway. If all else failed a wagon could be moved by using brute strength and a pinch bar (a stout wooden pole with a metal wedge end) that was jammed under the wheel tread and then raised to initiate motion.

Many of the pictures I did take caught, not always intentionally, platelayers at work. There were no protective clothes or fluorescent jackets, just picks and shovels. Even so, track alignments were often superb. Fishplates, usually with four bolts, were used to join rails together before the days of continuous welded rail. The joints got a fearful hammering and a familiar sight was that of a figure bent over a fishplate with a metal can of heavy oil, a long-handled brush and an equally long-handled spanner to tighten the bolts.

On stations, in signal boxes and in goods yards and depots there were many other competent railwaymen at work using dedicated and extensive skills, albeit in ways that now seem almost primitive. It is humbling to think of how much we took for granted, even the brutal, hard and dangerous skills that are now lost for ever.

NORTH AMERICAN INTERLUDE

────◄○►────

Jim White made a decision that transported him from a relief clerk post at Dumfries to the US and Canada

I joined BR around April 1954 as a junior clerk in the parcels office at Dumfries station. I had left school on the Friday and started work on the following Monday in the middle of term having decided, rightly or wrongly, that I had sufficient education for my needs. After nine months, like all other 18-year-olds in those days, I was called up for National Service and was selected to spend my two years in the Royal Air Force, appropriately enough as a 'Clerk, Movements'. My two years passed relatively uneventfully, having been posted to 16MU, RAF Stafford, conveniently on the west coast route to Scotland.

On demobilisation I returned to BR and took up a position as a relief clerk based at Dumfries and covering the area from Annan to Auchinleck on the old Glasgow & South Western Railway Main Line and Stranraer town on the 'Port Road'. Learning was very much an 'on the job' exercise, as returnees from National Service were given just two fortnight refresher courses at Dunbar, one each on passenger and freight commercial activities. As my nine months' previous experience had been limited to parcels work my knowledge base was fairly limited, as evidenced by each time I had to attempt to fill in the sack return at New Cumnock, a document designed to challenge a PhD in maths.

The next two and a half years passed uneventfully, spent at stations now long gone or with vastly reduced services. Then, one afternoon, I was on the late shift at Dumfries booking office when I took a call from the staff section of the district traffic office at Ayr. The clerk explained that a request had been received to submit names of possible candidates to work for nine months in the Toronto office of British & Irish Railways (a joint operation of BR and the two Irish railway undertakings Córas Iompair Éireann [CIÉ] and UTA). The caller asked whether there were any suitable staff in Dumfries who met the criteria of having booking and enquiry experience, being single and also being Scottish.

Going through my colleagues rapidly in my head I replied that I thought not, but was then asked about a relief clerk named White. Confirming my identity, I agreed to have my name included, a decision that was life changing, although I did not know it at the time. I then forgot about the conversation, confident in my own mind that such an attractive posting would go to someone with good connections in the corridors of power.

Some months later, while working at Annan, I was summoned to an interview at the BRB headquarters in Marylebone Road, an adventure of considerable importance when compared to my usual round of activities. Having met some of the other candidates I returned home convinced that I could forget about the position so far as I was concerned.

Christmas and New Year came and went until, in February, I was working at Stranraer when the staff office tracked me down and a voice enquired whether I had a passport. On replying in the negative I was asked if I could obtain one and be on the *Queen Mary* sailing for New York in ten days' time at the end of February. I responded affirmatively and was duly on the ship when she sailed for Cherbourg and the wide Atlantic, along with four other BR and CIÉ clerks heading for the B&I offices in New York, Los Angeles, Chicago and Toronto.

In those days BR had an arrangement with Cunard that allowed staff on business to travel at reduced fares in the best cabins in steerage class. On that voyage the ship was pretty full and our contingent was placed in two-berth cabins below the waterline and just above the engines. I was seasick from the Bay of Biscay until we neared the US coastline.

On disembarking we were met in the cavernous luggage hall by Peter Green from the B&I New York permanent staff who escorted us to the office, located in those days in the Rockefeller Centre at 630 Fifth Avenue, a prestigious address. I was not permitted to dally in the city, however, and that night found myself on the overnight train to Toronto, my destination for the next nine months. I was allowed a couple of night's hotel accommodation until I found a room in 'Dizzie's Doss House', as it was affectionately known. This was a boarding house run by an English lady (a pre-war motor-racing driver), who provided bed and board for about half a dozen, mainly British, guests.

The background to my new activity lay in the establishment of a representative office in New York by the LMS in 1937 – not the best of timing in view of subsequent events. During the Second World War the office was maintained by one redoubtable lady, apparently virtually unaided, until tourism started to flourish when peace returned. By 1960 the pressure on staff in the peak summer months necessitated additional resources, hence the transfer of one experienced clerk to each of the four North American offices. Due to the historical links between Canada and Scotland the majority of Canadian tourists were including Scotland in their itineraries, hence the request for a relief clerk from the Scottish Region to come to the Toronto office.

The work was interesting, which included issuing tickets (mainly against orders received from travel agents) and dealing with Britrail passes and Thrift coupons, rail and ferry services and enquiries from the various agents, airlines and members of the public. In addition to the railway companies and all ferry services, B&I also represented the hotels of its constituents, plus the Trust House and Grand Metropolitan Hotel chain and also several large coach-touring companies, enabling complete package holidays to be put together.

In the May a notable event occurred for me when the chief clerk recruited a new secretary who was to play a significant role in my life. Nevertheless, October eventually came around and my time in Toronto came to an end. I found myself back on the *Queen Mary* heading for Southampton, although this time I was free from *mal de mer* for the entire crossing and enjoyed a single cabin boasting its own porthole.

On my return, and without any interval, I was back on relief in my old position, my first job being at Thornhill Goods where a wet October Monday morning found me walking round the yard noting down the numbers of wagons shunted in over the weekend. With the rain running down the back of my BR waterproof and my notebook becoming ever more sodden, I debated whether it would have been wiser to resign when in Canada and become a permanent immigrant!

THE RETURN

————◁◯▷————

An unexpected telephone call took Jim White back to Canada
and later to the United States

Having enjoyed a summer of working in Toronto the return to south-west
Scotland was a considerable contrast. Then, when I was covering the late shift
at Stranraer one day in late January 1961, I received a call from Regional
Headquarters in Glasgow asking whether I was prepared to return to Toronto
the following month for another nine months there. Needless to say, I did not
hesitate, and February once again found me on the boat train to Southampton
where the *Queen Mary* was waiting to take me and the other relief clerks to
New York and, in my case, thence by train to Toronto.

As the months passed it became apparent that a significant and growing
amount of revenue was originating from the western provinces of Canada,
notably British Columbia, which was some 3,000 miles and 3 hours time
difference away. After due consideration, the BRB agreed that an office
should be opened there with the proviso that a target revenue should be
reached within three years. I was appointed as clerk in the new office and it
was agreed that I should drive out west, with expenses of 10 cents per mile
to cover my costs. The trip on the still-under-construction Trans-Canada
Highway took ten days and meant covering 3,600 miles in total.

After two years on the west coast and with the financial target already met,
I was promoted to sales representative in the New York office and responsible
for covering the southern states from Washington DC, south to Miami and
west through Texas – a considerable area and, in my opinion, the best sales
job on BR.

The customer base was primarily travel agents, the pattern being to
spend the winter on the road and the summer looking after one's customers
in the office. For me this translated into taking the 'Peach Queen' train
from Pennsylvania station to Raleigh or thereabouts, covering Virginia
and the Carolinas by car, flying to Miami and then working my way north
to Jacksonville. As I included Daytona Beach in my itinerary I took the
opportunity to drive along the sands there, famous as the home of many
land-speed record attempts.

From Jacksonville the overnight train delivered me the next morning to New Orleans to cover that city and Baton Rouge, then off on another flight to Houston. On one visit to Houston I was asked to give a 10-minute radio talk on the forthcoming 'Flying Scotsman' service. I was still talking at the end of the 10 minutes and was asked to return the next week. I then did further spots for this programme, which was syndicated to some 200 local radio stations across the USA.

On another visit to Houston on a hot, sunny day in November, I was returning to my hotel when I ran into stationary traffic. On walking to the head of the queue I was in time to see President Kennedy, his wife and entourage drive past in an open car. The next day I was driving to Dallas via Waco when, on setting off around 12.30 p.m., I switched on the radio to hear that a few minutes earlier President Kennedy had been assassinated and was being rushed to hospital. I stopped in Waco but no one was interested in anything but the events in Dallas so I pressed on to my hotel there.

The following day was a Saturday and, on leaving my hotel for a walk, I noticed a crowd of people standing on the opposite corner of the street. Having nothing better to do I joined them and discovered that I was outside the jail where Lee Harvey Oswald was being held before being moved to another secure location. Just then my neighbour asked, 'Did you hear that?' But I had not. It was the sound of a gunshot, of Jack Ruby killing Oswald.

The whole area then erupted. An ambulance arrived, was too large to fit into the tunnel under the jail and was replaced by a smaller one which took Oswald off, already dead. With Monday being declared a day of mourning and few people interested in considering UK travel plans, I called short my trip and returned to New York. Since then I have read extensively about the assassination of JFK and returned once to Dallas where I stood on the famous 'Grassy Knoll'. I remain of the view that Oswald was not working alone, but I doubt we shall ever really know.

The rest of my career on BR was somewhat less exciting than this period. I had returned to the UK to become a TA in Scotland. In January 1968 I was appointed a salesman in International Container Services, that very individualistic organisation in Finsbury Square, London within the Shipping Division of BR and which launched the first lift on–lift off container service between Harwich and Zeebrugge. But that is another story in itself.

DERAILMENTS

————◄◊►————

As David Barraclough's narrative demonstrates, derailments
were a fact of railway life

Wath Yard

'How many off; how many buffer-locked?' This was often the first question
the incoming assistant yardmaster at Wath yard asked of the assistant yardmaster
he was relieving. It was a crucial question as it frequently determined one's
activities for part, hopefully, or even most of the shift. Pushing an average
of 3,000 wagons over the yard's 'A' and 'B' humps every 24 hours was not
going to be achieved if either or both of these two problems caused any of
the thirty sorting sidings beyond each hump to become blocked. An assistant
yardmaster's first priority was to keep the throughput of wagons flowing
over the humps and if either derailment or buffer-locking hindered this the
'pilot' – a 350hp radio-fitted diesel – and a human shunter would be needed
in a hurry.

Rerailing was usually simple: just set the ramp or ramps correctly and pull
the derailed vehicle up their incline, and usually 'on she went'. Buffer-locking
was even simpler, done by pulling the offending wagons to a siding split to
alter their alignment. Too easy, though, to proceed happily and fail to notice
that one wagon could be buffer-locked in the opposite direction to another
one or even buffer-locked at both ends so that the change in direction
produced a derailment.

On my shift I had a yard foreman who was very keen on closing up
wagons on the sorting sidings below the hump. This was something that had
to be done slowly without the wagons being attached to the pilot and with
sufficient handbrakes applied. Slow and steady was the rule. One afternoon
there were several sidings below 'A' hump to be pushed down and this
became less than slow and steady. On an adjacent 'B' hump siding a Mottram
train was just departing when my foreman pushed too hard, resulting in
buffering-up and a heavy collision with the wagons of the departing train.
Thirteen wagons were derailed and an overhead electric supply mast brought

down with the 1,500V dc wires falling across the departing train and tripping the supply. The Mottram guard was shaken but thankfully unharmed. Three hours had been wasted in putting matters right and one siding was out of use for four days.

On another occasion the carriage and wagon examiner on duty called me to come down to a siding off 'B' hump where he said there was a derailment. We met and there was a recently repaired and repainted Lowmac wagon that was en route to an industrial firm in Rotherham who had purchased it from BR. The wagon was not derailed in the strict sense of the term. As a result of a very rough shunt one pair of wheels and half the length of the wagon was upside down on top of the other half, a situation that took some sorting out. We could drag the half wagon in one direction and in the end took it over 'B' hump and then pushed it, protesting, until we reached a spot where it was out of the way and could be cut up on site.

All this excitement occurred during my ten-month secondment to Wath, the ex-Great Central Railway yard built in 1907 and where some 3,000

Another train of empties for Wath yard passes beneath a loading gauge behind Robinson Class 01 2-8-0 locomotive No. 63727. (Bryan Stone)

1-ton mineral wagons were sorted every day in the 1960s and even on into the '70s.

Doncaster Division

The Doncaster Division of BR was bisected by the East Coast Main Line and had a number of branches of some importance. Within broad boundaries of Spalding–Seamer and Mansfield–Cleethorpes it dealt with many passenger services and just over 22 per cent of the whole of the BR freight traffic. Until August 1973 a significant portion of the latter was ironstone for the Scunthorpe blast furnaces coming from an area south-west of Grantham at Sproxton and Stainby (the Highdyke branch off the East Coast Main Line) and the Denton branch off the Grantham–Nottingham line.

The iron-ore content of this home-mined ore was only 15 per cent and this necessitated the running of five Class 6 fully fitted trains of thirty-five 'Tipfit' wagons and seven unfitted trains of up to fifty tipplers five days each week and up to seven trains on Saturdays. The unfitted services alone conveyed 1,500 tons per train, 56,900 tons each week. The services were all worked by Grantham train crews on an out and home basis with routings at various times via Honington, Newark and then to Doncaster via Crowle. The unfitted trains originally ran via the East Lincs line and then via Newark and Barnetby. They were later upgraded to Class 7 with a vacuum-fitted portion of additional brake power.

Over the years only two derailments stand out. One was on a Saturday evening in the depths of winter when a broken rail near Worlaby on top of the North Lincolnshire Wolds resulted in twenty wagons out of the thirty-five on a Class 6 train being derailed and turning on their sides on top of the low embankment. It was bitterly cold and freezing outside with snowflakes blowing in the wind. The clearing up would have to wait but by crowding all the attending departments into the warm signal box and sending the locomotive crew back to the warmth of their Class 47 diesel we were able to complete the paperwork in record time, which would avoid the need for a divisional inquiry.

The other ironstone derailment occurred late one sunny morning when a Class 7 Highdyke–Frodingham train was passing over Boultham level crossing on the approach to Lincoln St Marks station. The cause was eventually found on site to be a broken axle on one of the unfitted tippler wagons in the train, many wagons of which went all over the place and, in doing so, managed to fracture the main underground gas pipe that supplied the greater part of Lincoln. The escaping gas caught fire with a dramatic flame rising some 30ft in the air. The local fire service was quickly on site and gave instructions that the flame must continue to burn to avoid an explosion and that under no circumstances should an attempt be made to extinguish the fire until the gas had been cut off on both sides of the level crossing. BR staff were permitted to begin sorting out the shambles within 30 minutes and use of the Immingham and Doncaster steam cranes was also approved.

An old lady living in a bungalow just south of the level crossing agreed to the use of her telephone for emergency communications; the guard of the train had already protected the rear and the locomotive second man the front. The guard's journal showed forty-nine wagons but a count down the wreckage could only account for forty-six. We then found two adjacent wagons, one of which was attached to its neighbour but buried with only the top 6in visible. Where was the forty-ninth wagon? We eventually found it crushed between two tipplers and reduced to a total width of 18in!

The cause of the accident lay with the nineteenth wagon. The axle was in two parts and had been detached from the frame and tossed to the side of the track. It took nearly three days to clear up the whole mess and repair the

Lincoln St Marks station looking towards Boultham Junction where the avoiding line diverges south to cross this main road into Lincoln city centre.

track, and yet another day before it was safe enough to turn off the burning gas and replace the fractured main.

The fire service also attended a derailment that occurred at Crowle one autumn weekend. After weekend engineering work replacing a crossover just west of the station, the first train to pass on the Monday morning was one from Ince & Elton–Normanby Park conveying eighteen loaded 100-ton French-built tank wagons loaded with liquid ammonia under a pressure of 20psi and destined for the Flixborough agricultural fertiliser works. In the middle of the train the rear bogie of one wagon had derailed in the crossover and become buffer locked with the adjacent tankers.

The Immingham 36-ton crane was despatched immediately to the site, with the Doncaster 75-ton crane arriving there some 50 minutes later. The lie of the derailed tanker prevented the Immingham crane being able to reach and lift it, so the smaller crane was returned to base after removing the buffers from one end of the tanker so that the adjoining ones could be drawn clear. The Doncaster crane did a similar job at the other end to allow a spreader beam to be placed under the buffer beam, as these tankers had no through underframe.

The task of lifting the tanker began but had to be abandoned when the spreader frame started to bend. Instead 50-ton jacks were set up on packing on either side of the tanker and a successful lift was achieved. What to do next? The decision was taken to remove the jack on one side to allow the bogie to sink down to near rail alignment and then rebuild the packing with a final lift to rerail. It became clear that knocking out the supporting jack might not be easy, but among the Doncaster breakdown crew there was a large and tall man weighing 18 stone whose personal strength had been used before in such situations. He was to take the big, long-handled, heavy hammer and take a mighty swing at the jack. The Crowle fire-service team leader who was on spot was consulted and he advised his team of the position and told them that if anything went wrong they should dive into the deep drain on the left of the running lines or the Sheffield–Keadby canal on the right!

The decisive moment came and we all stood back, the firemen retreating to a safe distance to watch the event. Walter, the strong man, took the hammer, swung it fiercely and the left-hand jack flew out. The bogie of the tanker settled down to within an inch of the rail. We glanced up to see all the firemen, except the leader, sprinting as fast as they could go towards Crowle station. Afterwards they expressed their views as to the sanity of the assembled railwaymen!

A simple lift and the tanker was back on the rails. The permanent-way inspector had done his measuring and determined that the relayed crossover was 'tight to gauge', causing the derailment. Carefully the damaged vehicle and the rear end of the ammonia train were drawn clear of the crossover by a Class 47 locomotive and taken slowly back to Crowle station to await further examination, and the tension slowly drained from those involved.

MORE DERAILMENTS

Although no longer his direct responsibility in Scotland, David Barraclough still attended a number of derailments

In between my time at Wath in 1961–62 and my return to the Doncaster Division in August 1968 I spent three years in Glasgow based in the Hope Street operations hub of the division, and was occasionally able to attend incidents in the more rural parts of the territory. One such incident was a derailment at the trap points off the branch from Muirkirk behind the signal box at Auchinleck in Ayrshire. The Ayr Harbour–Falkland Junction trip to Kaimes Colliery at Muirkirk was returning behind a Class 25 locomotive with a full load of export coal but failed to stop at the trap points protecting the Glasgow & South Western Main Line, derailing the locomotive and three wagons.

As we approached the scene a colliery 'Pug' shunting locomotive was seen proceeding back towards Muirhead bunker and hauling ten or so loaded coal wagons – very strange! What became clear was that it had become the practice for the morning trip to clear all the loaded wagons from the colliery if by doing so a second trip in the afternoon could be avoided. This had meant that the derailed working was eight wagons over the maximum loading, resulting in the driver being unable to halt his train as it approached the main line.

As soon as the mishap occurred the signal box had advised the pit, which had then promptly sent the Pug down with the intention of clearing the excess wagons from the rear of the casualty in order to hide the evidence of overloading. But it was not quick enough over the 12 miles from Kaimes to Auchinleck box and, in any event, there would have been nowhere to hide those offending wagons and so the story came out!

Not too long later, in early 1967, there was another incident in the same area, this time along the line from Newton-on-Ayr–Mauchline Junction, which had a long branch from Annbank Junction–Killoch Colliery. The latter's daily order for 'Minfits' (16-ton vacuum brake-fitted coal wagons) could be as high as 360 wagons and it was the new practice to concentrate all of these wagons there as was possible. By the Saturday before the accident Killoch was full of such wagons.

On the Monday the Falkland Junction trip was returning down the gradient of the branch towards Annbank headed by two Class 20 locomotives and with a full load – mostly loaded Minfits plus a few unfitted 16-tonners (residue from the previous week) – at the rear. The driver braked on the approach to Annbank but, unfortunately, forgot that most of his train was piped up to the locomotives giving him considerable braking capacity. This resulted in his train stopping dead within a very short distance, much as if it had hit a cliff head on. Wagons, both fitted and unfitted, jumped all over the place, mostly not on the rails, and quite a few finished upside down or on their sides.

The driver held his hand up for the chaos he had caused and it took two days to clear things up. The new working arrangements went well thereafter and within weeks we were able to introduce two trains a day, with Ayr men working through Glasgow to Cadder yard with fully fitted loads of coal for Edinburgh, Stirling, Perth and the north via the City Union link, which had never before in its many years been used for regular through traffic movements.

Lastly, something completely different. At Corpach, just beyond the Caledonian canal and just outside Fort William on the line to Mallaig, Wiggins Teape Ltd had established a pulp mill which, in addition to its normal incoming timber traffic, also received 45-ton, two-axle tanks of fuel oil for the works.

One lunchtime the area manager at Fort William rang the Hope Street office to say that one of these oil tanks had imploded and become derailed in the mill sidings. What to do? We called in our Carriage and Wagon colleagues and they set out to investigate. They discovered that the mill shunter had failed to release the air valve on the tank. As a result, as the oil was being discharged to the static storage tank, the suction action drew the body of the tank inwards with the resulting imbalance causing one pair of wheels to come off the track.

Not Ayrshire, but a typical derailment presenting one easy re-railing job, but with those beyond the 'Stop' board presenting more of a challenge.

The re-railing was effected but the damaged tank had to be cut up on site for scrap, with Wiggins Teape making a financial settlement to its owners and the fuel oil suppliers. Not the usual type of mishap though.

IT CAN NOW BE REVEALED

―――◄○►―――

Being helpful is not always without its problems, as Philip Benham discovered at York

As one of Britain's most impressive large stations, York has often been used as a period film set. It featured in the 1979 film *Agatha* about the disappearance of the famous crime writer Agatha Christie, and more recently was used for scenes in one of the 'Harry Potter' films, masquerading as King's Cross no less.

In 1983, while I was area manager, the station was also chosen for a sequence in the film *The Dresser*. With a star cast including Albert Finney, Tom Courtney and Edward Fox, the plot was based around a travelling theatre company during the Second World War. York's part was to play another station (I was told it was supposed to be Carlisle) where the troupe were changing trains, leading to one of the film's most memorable lines uttered by Albert Finney, 'Stop that train!'

Quite a bit of advance work was needed to prepare the location and secure appropriate carriages that could be made to look the part, and also to hire a couple of LMS Railway steam engines – Pacific *Duchess of Hamilton* and 'Black 5', No. 5407. A couple of lightly used platforms in the 'Scarborough corner' at the north-east of the station were allocated for the filming, well out of harm's way. These were also conveniently close to 'Tearoom Square' where the film crew could park their vehicles and set up catering facilities – well over a hundred extras were being hired in addition to the cast and production team, so feeding was a big issue. George Hinchcliffe from the Carnforth Steamtown preservation centre had been appointed to liaise between the film team and the railway, and I asked the York station manager Jim Collins to look after the operational arrangements. Meanwhile the film company had acquired a number of withdrawn Mark 1 coaches and engaged a painter who spent many days repainting them into LMS maroon to fit the film's period.

Come the morning for the filming, everything seemed set up. The coaches had been placed in one of the bay platforms the day before, the two steam locos had arrived from the National Railway Museum where they had been lit up and prepared, the extras had arrived in a couple of road coaches and the cast were ready. There was even a chair with the words 'Albert Finney' on the back! The plan was to load the cast and the extras into the coaches, which the 'Black 5' would then propel out of the station to the River Ouse Bridge on the Scarborough line. It would then draw back into the station as an arriving train, with the extras creating the scene of a crowd of passengers getting off the train after it had stopped.

In my office the phone rang, it was Jim. 'Would you come over to the station, as there is a slight problem?' Across I went to hear that it had just been discovered that none of the carefully painted coaches had any working brakes as, being withdrawn for scrapping, all the vacuum pipes and other brake equipment had been removed. This was indeed a big problem, as it is a fundamental rule stretching back to the nineteenth century that passenger trains must have automatic brakes controlled from the locomotive.

So what was to be done? BR had sold the coaches to the film company and, of course, was also being paid handsomely for their services. While there seemed to have been some breakdown in communication, it was clear that if filming could not take place then there was to be a huge amount at stake.

'Coronation' 4-6-2 locomotive No. 6229 *Duchess of Hamilton* stands in the 'Scarborough Corner' of York station with the coaches used in the film *The Dresser*. (Philip Benham)

Actors, extras, all would have to be stood down, while rescheduling could take weeks, bearing in mind the need to obtain more carriages and dovetail with the diaries of the actors. Quite apart from the cost, the production schedule for the whole film would be thrown into disarray.

After a hasty conference with Jim, George and Regional Public Affairs who had let the film contract, I agreed that as we were talking about one low-speed movement of less than a ¼ of a mile the film sequence could take place under certain conditions. In particular the driver was to be instructed to take great care, proceeding at little more than walking pace as he drew the train into the station. The film director was to understand that there would be one take only, so his cameramen had better get it right first time.

Everyone was duly briefed and the train sent back. Cameras were in position, the director gave the nod for the train to start, the driver whistled acknowledgement for the tip from the guard and opened the regulator on No. 5407. Observing from the platform Jim and I saw a huge column of smoke emerge from 5407's chimney as the train eagerly leapt forward.

We looked at each other nervously, fearing trouble. The train entered the platform at a speed which to me suggested a liberal interpretation of the words 'walking pace'. It kept on coming until the speed finally began to drop, but unfortunately not quite fast enough, as the engine reached the end of the line and nudged into the buffer stops with a bang. Having checked that no one was hurt, down on to the track Jim and I both went to see if there had been any damage. The engine appeared fine, but the buffer stops had been moved a few inches and were severed from the rails.

For my part I felt distinctly uncomfortable, but the film director had what he wanted, so hopefully that would be that. Unfortunately I hadn't counted on Miles Kington being there, a journalist who at the time wrote a regular humorous column in *The Times*. About a week after the incident his next piece appeared under the heading 'Waiting for Train'. 'I have just seen a real train crash at York,' he started, going on to describe in embarrassing detail what had happened, including reference to the 'two fat controllers in bowler hats' who had gone down to have a look (actually Jim is rather slim).

Ready for her part in *The Dresser* film, Stanier ex-LMS 4-6-0 No. 5407 is pictured in front of the buffer stops she was later to unseat. (Philip Benham)

This was alarming, especially as daily press cuttings from all the papers were circulated to the regional headquarters senior officers. An urgent call was made to Regional Public Affairs Manager Bert Porter. Fortunately when General Manager Frank Paterson picked up the item it was to Bert that he directed a query, who was able to tell him, 'Don't worry, General Manager, it's all been dealt with.' Had the question gone to the regional operations officer, his response might have been rather different!

There was an interesting sequel. One of the other scenes involved the theatre troupe being filmed running over the station footbridge. Clearing the footbridge of all passengers during the working day had been quite a logistical challenge, as were the special effects to create an impression of smoke and steam. Some months later when the film was released, a number of us were invited to a special screening at the National Museum of Photography, Film and Television in Bradford. We eagerly awaited the station scenes and then watched with interest as the troupe made their wartime dash over the footbridge just as an InterCity High Speed Train passed by underneath!

THE PAY RUN

————◄○►————

*What seemed like an easy job for Ian Body didn't quite
turn out that way*

In the mid '70s I had a period in the management team based at Exeter St David's, and being relatively young and naïve I was unanimously chosen to undertake the weekly pay run. This was an activity carried out every Thursday, primarily to distribute pay for those members of staff who could not receive theirs from a booking office or from the central pay office at Exeter. Thus it was largely built around a variety of far-flung signal boxes and smaller stations. At the outset it seemed like a rather cushy number – being given the company Mini for a few hours and being let loose in the pleasant Devon countryside – how hard could that be?

On the first occasion of going out my initial cause to draw breath was when I collected the wage packets for which I would be responsible for during the next few hours. I had overlooked that each delivery point would receive wage packets for all three shifts and for all staff based there, together with some other groups of staff who chose to use them as their collection point. This meant that some eighty wage packets were involved which, at today's values, would represent at least £50,000! When the accounts clerk said 'sign here' my signature was somewhat more shaky than normal.

The second element of surprise was being sent round to the stores office before departure. I had glibly assumed that 'pay run' meant just that – but oh no! My delivery round was the only way to distribute the myriad of tools and domestic items that kept the outlying locations running, so gradually the Mini began to resemble the classic game on Crackerjack where contestants had to hold on to everything they won. Everything from broom handles, lamp wicks, signalmen's dusters, detonators, collars, flags and Bardic lamps to pencil sharpeners, receipt books, carbon paper, letter spikes and coal scuttles found their way into the car's small boot and the back seat. Add in the weekly operating notices for each calling point and I was ready to go.

I had been bright enough to have spent some time in advance working out a suitable route to ensure that I could arrive at my last point of call just before 2 p.m. to avoid missing the early turn staff and incurring their wrath as they waited for me and potentially missed their lunch.

So off I went. First stop Exminster signal box to the west to get this out of the way quickly before turning back east and heading for Whimple, Feniton and then Honiton. At this point it then required a longer driving stint to Cowley Bridge Junction where the Barnstaple branch left the West of England Main Line. Then it was north to Crediton with my route planning working faultlessly. But next on the list was Salmon Pool Crossing with wages and provisions for the crossing keeper. What on paper should have taken about 20 minutes in fact took just over an hour with visits to far more farm tracks, dead ends and even quite deep fords than I had intended. Now I was really up against it as far as Tiverton Junction was concerned for that critical 2 p.m. arrival.

Stoke Canon signal box went to plan, as did Hele & Bradninch, although it was a delicate balancing act between genuine speed and the need to avoid giving offence by taking up the offer of a cup of tea at every single stopping point. Sadly my system could not cope with the constant topping up with tea, which then necessitated a detour to a local filling station for my benefit rather than that of the car.

The result was that arrival at Tiverton Junction was not going to be on time; indeed, it turned out to be 2.30 p.m., which I didn't think was too bad for a first attempt and at least I would only be inconveniencing one early turn signalman. Not until my arrival did I remember that this was where a further twenty members of the permanent-way gang came for their money, and so I was met by twenty-one angry men, mostly 'armed' with 4ft-fishplate spanners and shovels and all blaming me for their delayed meals.

What had originally seemed an inconvenience at having the final delivery to the small freight point of Uffculme now proved a miraculous escape route and at last I could calm down and slow down. It was never quite as hectic as that first time, as I became far more knowledgeable of short cuts and was gradually trusted to transfer all variety of unofficial items between signal boxes for staff personal purposes (I didn't ask!).

WINTERINGHAM AND FRODINGHAM

———◦———

Bill Parker got a military-style briefing for a task he was given at Doncaster

In late 1949 after National Service, I returned to the Doncaster district superintendent's office and a job in the passenger-train section. The following summer I was appointed to a low-grade summer relief stationmaster post and this was extended throughout the following winter. In practice I spent my time split between the passenger trains office and relieving stationmasters, an arrangement that the head of the office was, understandably, not over-keen on. However, it suited me splendidly, as getting involved with the sharp end of railway activity was a useful contrast with my district office job of passenger-train planning, special working and punctuality.

I recall in the late autumn being summoned by the assistant district operating superintendent who, along with a number of other senior railway managers at that period, retained his wartime curt military manner. Somewhat like addressing a subaltern I was told to sit down, but before I could was asked, 'Do you know where Winteringham and Winterton & Thealby are? Have you ever been there?'

I replied, 'Yes, sir,' to the first question and, 'No, sir,' to the second.

My orders followed, 'Well, that is where you are going next week to cover the stationmaster's leave. You stay in a modest hotel in Scunthorpe. Take your bike and your winter woollies.' A grin, and, 'It is only 8 miles to Winteringham and it gets b— cold on the Humber. But you may get a ride on a light engine if you can persuade the assistant yardmaster. Go to Scunthorpe on Sunday so you can oversee the ferry's departure on Monday. And while you are there, check the working at the two chutes used for coal and slag; keep an eye on the farmers and their sugar-beet traffic at Winterton, and the wagon use and demurrage charges. And I want an independent assessment of an earlier report about the future of the branch; involve the stationmaster who will be at home at the end of the week. Any questions? No? Good.'

Barely a pause and then, 'There is not much entertainment in Scunthorpe in the evenings apart from cinemas, pubs and the railway staff club. I want you to spend several hours in the evenings in Frodingham yard with the assistant yardmaster, yard inspectors and shunters. The yardmaster has been alerted. Fix the arrangements with him.'

K1 Class 2-6-0 No. 62063 heads a freight trip from Frodingham to Winteringham. (Bryan Stone)

Another pause for breath. 'You know the working at Wath and Doncaster yards marshalling already; I want a report from you on what you find out at Frodingham – for my eyes only!' Another grin. 'You're an acting, unpaid district freight inspector. Any questions? No? Off you go then.'

I felt I should salute, about turn and march out. As I opened the office door the final comments were, 'Enjoy yourself and be careful. See me in a fortnight with your reports.'

Despite this forbidding brief the assignment proved interesting and worthwhile. In my evenings at Frodingham I learned a considerable amount about the railway's steel operations and the arrangements with the steel companies. I did cycle to Winteringham on the Monday morning and found the bike very useful on those occasions during my assignment when I did not get a ride on a light engine or on the daily freight trip. And I also managed to get to the staff club late each evening before closing time for a drink and the inevitable quizzing as to what I was up to.

Conniving with the yardmaster, I included in my report several train working and minor track changes that he wanted. What subsequently happened to them I do not know. There was no feedback but I always got a friendly greeting on subsequent visits to Frodingham. The line beyond Winterton was closed the following year.

ROYAL MOMENTS

————◄◦►————

Royal travel was always a special occasion, as Philip Benham's experiences reveal

Whenever members of the royal family travelled by train the local area managers had to keep a weather eye on arrangements to ensure all went to plan. If the royal person was joining or alighting at one of your stations either the area manager in person or one of his assistants had to be in attendance. Even if the royal train was merely passing through the patch, there were management tasks to perform, particularly if the train was booked to stop for a crew change, in which case a check was needed to ensure a smooth handover, and also to see that the relieving crew were suitably attired in their best uniform. Often the crew would have been specially selected, with royal duties generally highly regarded and assigned to senior men. If need be this could even be the excuse for a fresh uniform issue.

My first involvement with the royal train as a young assistant area manager was to supervise just such a crew change at Leicester. The identity of the royal personage is lost in the mists of time but hardly mattered since the exchange was in the small hours when all sensible people including, hopefully, 'The Principal' (as the royal passenger was invariably referred to) would have been fast asleep. Despite all the details having being set out in a special notice issued on a 'need to know' basis some days before, it appeared that the one person who most definitely needed to know had not been told. This was the driver rostered to take the train forward from Leicester. When he arrived for duty his appearance was, let us just say, less than ideal, with no tie or even a proper jacket. With the earnestness of youth I let him know in no uncertain terms what I thought. His response suggested he was not a royalist as he expressed his opinion about the royal train, idiot managers and me in particular before threatening to book off duty. Fortunately the depot supervisor came to my rescue with an apology to the driver, explaining that he had not been told beforehand, and a spare tie and a jacket. Honour was saved and I learned a lesson in staff diplomacy.

The next royal encounter was more personal when, as area manager, I had to escort HRH Princess Anne on to a train at York in 1983. This was a private journey and she was joining a normal InterCity 125 High Speed Train for King's Cross. Unfortunately the train was running late and, as she was travelling alone, I had to keep the Princess entertained for about half an hour, including finding somewhere private for her to wait. Fortunately I was able to commandeer my assistant's office close to where the train would arrive, but what to talk about, as the Princess's plainclothes policeman had decided to leave me to it. I need not have worried for, of course, members of the royal family spend their lives talking to people. This was during Princess Anne's competitive horse-riding days and I recall learning quite a bit about eventing and show jumping.

The train finally arrived and as it departed, my duties complete, I walked back down the platform with the local BT police inspector, Brian Mennell. As the rear-power car roared past us, the platform supervisor remarked that he had just seen a passenger get into the rear of the train carrying what looked like a rifle. Brian reacted with horror but also instantly used his radio to alert the policeman on the train. Enquiries were made and it transpired that an American gentleman was off on the next stage of his fishing holiday!

Princess Anne came to York station again in 1985, but this was to be an altogether more prestigious affair. The centrepiece of her visit was the naming of a High Speed Train (HST) power car *Royal Signals*, a regiment of which I believe she was commander-in-chief. General Manager Frank Paterson officiated at the naming ceremony, with my supporting role being to present the Princess with a model of the named HST. Also present was the Lady Mayoress for York, Ruth Milner, whose father William had been killed searching for first-aid supplies while serving as a foreman at York station on the night of the 'Baedeker' air raid in 1942. Ruth had unveiled a commemorative plaque on the station the previous year. After the formal ceremony Frank invited the Princess to meet the two drivers. As Frank recalls, one quipped that he had lost a lot of money backing one of her mother's horses the previous week, to which the Princess replied, 'More fool you for wasting your money!' A very happy meeting then followed with station and area staff in the intimate setting of The Oak Room of the Royal York Hotel.

There were various other royal duties during my time at York, including a visit to Hull by the Prince and Princess of Wales using the royal train. The train duly arrived at Paragon station, but the Prince and Princess had separate engagements and it was Charles who alighted first. As always he was very enthusiastic about his journey overnight on the train, which had gone well. A short while later Diana left the train. She too was very polite and friendly, but had evidently not enjoyed the journey as much. 'We only use the train because Charles is a rail buff,' she said.

My move to be area manager at King's Cross in 1986 would lead to even more royal meetings. When the royal train was being used for an official royal visit, a regular routine would be for the train to leave the relevant London station late the previous evening, travelling through the night hours. Often en route the train would be stabled at a suitably quiet spot some distance from the final destination before completing the final stage of the journey to arrive at the appointed hour. Protocol demanded that the area manager or his deputy should attend the departure.

Given the status of King's Cross as the starting point for much of the eastern side of England and Scotland, such royal journeys were a regular occurrence. As a result I met most members of the royal family, with the formalities often much more relaxed at such late hours of the night. This was particularly so with the younger royals, who would often arrive from an evening 'engagement' having clearly enjoyed themselves! On occasions, timekeeping could also go slightly awry – not that the train was likely to go without them.

During this period I had one royal appointment that was not to be. The Prince of Wales was scheduled to return from up country by royal train to King's Cross early on the morning of 16 October 1987. I had booked into the Great Northern Hotel at King's Cross for an early night in order to be on hand to greet the Prince at the appointed hour. Some hours later my pager went off (this being before the advent of mobile phones) and drowsily I leant out to put on the bedside light, but to no effect. I then became aware of a loud shrieking sound. Stumbling out of bed in the pitch black I made for the window to look out across a London in almost total darkness. My first thought was that perhaps war had broken out, but I soon realised that the noise was the wind, for this was the night of the 'Great Storm' that devastated much of southern England.

Having negotiated my way from the hotel room, I entered an eerily dark King's Cross station where only the red signal lamps at the platform ends, on standby power, were illuminated. I made my way to our Control Office in the West Side offices that was lit, somewhat appropriately, by a single hurricane lamp. Here the night duty controller had just had a call from his wife to say they had lost half the roof on their house! With a mixture of trees and overhead lines down in more than a dozen places, it was obvious that trains would not be going anywhere for some time. The next few hours were interesting to say the least, as gradually the winds eased and our engineering colleagues put the railway back together. In the midst of all this was the royal train attempting to make its way back to the capital. Eventually we got the train to Potters Bar where, after several hours and with winds abating slightly, it was deemed safe to rescue HRH by car.

Where the monarch herself was concerned, matters remained rather more formal and timekeeping was always precise. The logistics of one such journey, when both the Queen and Duke of Edinburgh were travelling, are etched in my memory. To allow direct road access close to the royal train, the practice at King's Cross was for it to normally depart from Platform 1 adjoining the cab rank road that existed before construction of the modern-day Platform '0' (an apparent nonsense imposed by the need to avoid major changes to signalling designations). The Queen would usually arrive at the station in a large limousine that, although a magnificent vehicle, had a poor turning circle. So in order to avoid having to do a U-turn out of York Way (the road that runs down the east side of King's Cross station) standing instructions to the royal chauffeur were to always arrive from the northern end of York Way, allowing an easy turn into the ramped access road down to the cab rank. Perhaps it was a relief chauffeur or a mistake by the police, but, for whatever reason, on this particular night the royal car arrived along York Way from the wrong direction, leaving the chauffeur with no choice but to negotiate the U-turn on to the cab rank access road. The inevitable happened and the limousine had to go backwards and forwards several times to make the turn. When the royal car had finally made it, the Duke was not happy and expressed his opinion in no uncertain terms. I was left in no doubt that it was the railway's fault for not having a better-designed station!

A happier memory is of a civic visit by the Queen and Duke of Edinburgh to commemorate the 750th anniversary of Peterborough cathedral. Peterborough was towards the northern end of my 'patch' and as it was only 76 miles from London it was not considered necessary to use the royal train. Instead the Queen and the Duke would travel in a reserved coach on a scheduled InterCity service from King's Cross. Through the kindness of Charles Swift, one of our drivers and also council leader for the City of Peterborough, my wife Lesley and I were not only to be presented to Her Majesty in the line-up at Peterborough station, but also to attend the civic luncheon that followed. Having only got married a month earlier, to be able to invite my new bride to lunch with the Queen was rather special.

There was to be just one slight and amusing sting in the tail. As I was to be in the line-up at Peterborough, I could not oversee the departure or even the arrival, so my deputy David Sutcliffe would do the honours at King's Cross and Station Manager Peter Keys would welcome Her Majesty on arrival at Peterborough. This being an ordinary train, there was no red carpet to worry about; the train arrived right on time and all appeared to be well. As the royal party proceeded down the line, there was a glimmer of recognition from the Duke of Edinburgh.

'You're railway aren't you?' he asked.

'Yes, Your Royal Highness,' I replied, wondering what was coming next.

'Those trucks,' he said, referring to a rake of parcels vans that had been placed on the adjoining line as a security screen. 'Get them cleaned!'

Judging by the look the Queen gave the Duke she was 'not amused' by the joke.

Fast forward a quarter of a century to 2013 where, during a hot summer, there had been a number of lineside fires caused by steam engines working

The royal train at Hull Paragon station after carrying the Prince and Princess of Wales. (Philip Benham)

special trains on Network Rail. As chairman of the Friends of the Museum I was in the National Railway Museum at York for the arrival of the Prince of Wales on the footplate of the A4 Class locomotive *Bittern*. The event was the bringing together of the six surviving A4 streamlined Pacifics to commemorate the 75th anniversary of the world speed record by one of them: *Mallard*. The museum director, Paul Kirkman, introduced me to the Prince, explaining my role to him and telling him that I was also managing director of the steam-worked North Yorkshire Moors Railway. The Prince expressed an interest in what I was doing now and the subject of steam engines and fires came up. I commented that because our railway passes through moorland, much of which belongs to the Duchy of Lancaster, we have to be careful not to set fire to his land. The Prince replied, 'No, that's not mine, the Lancaster lands belong to the Monarch!'

Nowadays the royal train itself seems to venture out less and less from its home at Wolverton in Buckinghamshire. This seems a shame as it brings an element of splendour and ceremony to the railway in an age when trains can seem rather bland. Long may it survive.

MERSEYSIDE REFLECTIONS

———◆◇◆———

Jan Glasscock went to Merseyside during a period of major
change and challenge

In September 1983 I moved from being Operating Officer West Coast South at Euston to the post of area manager at Liverpool. This was a new post as the Liverpool and Garston areas were to be combined that December. Fortunately, most of the consultation and appointments work had been done, so my initial task was to bring about the merger without detrimental effect on the operational railway. With the help of the two retiring area managers this task was completed on schedule with no major problems in the new area, which inherited some 800 staff.

I got an early feel for the sort of people I would be working with from the nickname the local staff had given my deputy, the operations manager. He had been at Liverpool for some years and had come from King's Cross where he was the assistant station manager. He was not afraid to tell staff how to run the job and frequently used the phrase 'when I was at the Cross' – the Cross being the term local people used when referring to King's Cross. Liverpudlians quickly latched on to this, saying that he had come down from the Cross and giving him the nickname 'JC', which stayed with him at Liverpool until his retirement.

Many changes happened around this time, including the conversion to merry-go-round working of the coal arriving at Garston Docks for shipment to Ireland and the Isle of Man. This involved a completely different method of working which required fewer local shunting locomotives and staff than had previously been the case. Some difficult meetings about the change took place with the local staff representatives who were not backward in telling their new area manager what they thought. At one meeting I was informed by the drivers' LDC that I was called 'The Smiling Assassin' and 'had done more damage around Garston than Hitler'. It did not help the temperature of the meeting when I responded, 'Yes, it took him four years; it's only taken me one!' The formal record of the meeting recorded that 'a full and frank exchange of views took place'. We did have a pint together on more than one occasion later once we had got to know one another better.

Another major change to come in was the Driver Only Operation (DOO) on freight trains, with Garston-Willesden Freightliners being one of three trial flows, along with iron ore in Scotland and South Wales. To the surprise of many, the Garston trains were the only ones to run. This was no mean achievement, brought about by the managers and inspectors on the ground at Garston who performed the shunting duties and the chief signalling inspector who made sure that any signalman who wavered over signalling a DOO freight train knew very clearly on which side his bread was buttered.

In the course of a difficult few weeks of change the local union branch secretary and I had a lengthy discussion after the local branch meeting. We agreed that although we could not agree professionally we would not fall out personally, upon which he invited me as his guest to an evening social event of the National Signallers Conference being held at nearby Southport. I was very pleased to accept, even if we did both get a few barbed comments from some of the 'brothers' there!

All areas have their 'characters' and Merseyside was no exception. Reading the personal file of one I was to see, along with his advocate, I was struck with its thickness. It was full of incidents such as crossing gates run through, side rods bent on an O8 Class diesel shunting locomotive due to excessive speed and a fusible plug dropped on a steam locomotive. The one that really caught my attention, however, was when he was driving a DMU to Manchester that had been seen by a signaller with the cab lights on and an Alsatian dog apparently driving it! The seven bells 'stop and examine' train signal was sent to the next signal box where the driver was found to be in the correct position. His version was that, living on his own, he did not want to leave the dog alone and so took it to work with him. When his Weekly Traffic Notice fell on the floor and he bent down to pick it up the dog jumped into his seat!

For the 1989 FA Cup Final between Liverpool and Everton we managed to run eighteen special trains including one VIP service for each of the teams. On paper this appeared impossible, but the local staff representatives indicated that we should do whatever was needed, even if out of the ordinary. Traction inspectors moved locomotives, guards worked stock from Downhill Sidings to Lime Street station and the departing train plan worked like clockwork with fans from both teams not needing to be segregated and willing to travel together.

Unfortunately, this was more than could be said about the return, which went badly wrong when one of the early services was stopped at Rugby as a result of a passenger pulling the communication cord. Later services then passed the halted train, resulting in their approach to Liverpool being in the wrong order and totally messing up the drivers' and guards' workings. Several services had to be terminated at Edge Hill and run empty into Downhill Sidings while others were seriously delayed into Lime Street. The next day one of the local radio presenters gave us praise for the trip to London but a resounding 'raspberry' for the return journey. We were 'guilty as charged'.

Another memorable member of the staff was a signaller at Edge Hill Power Box, who found a very imaginative way of preventing delays when a locomotive derailment meant putting in SLW between Wavertree Junction and Edge Hill station. He later had an excellent book published about his career in signal boxes in the north-west entitled *Sojourn of a Railway Signalman*, which I enjoyed despite its somewhat derogatory references to my train regulating abilities whilst working the Edge Hill Panel!

Not long after, I moved to the post of area manager at Crewe. I left Liverpool with many happy memories of the staff who had the success of the railway industry at heart. These included professional trade union representatives you could trust and do business with, but I guess that sums up the railway at most places in the country.

DANGEROUS GOODS

---◆---

An unusual publicity promotion presented Philip Benham with a startling challenge

Many years ago a well-known oil company used the advertising slogan 'Put a tiger in your tank' to promote the qualities of their petrol. Working in the Special Services section of the Nottingham division in 1971 the phrase took on a particular resonance for me, although mine was a different kind of 'big cat'.

In Special Services, which was part of the divisional passenger manager's office, we were charged with developing new promotions to generate extra business. One of these ideas was to offer a combined travel and entrance ticket for a day out to the new safari park recently opened at Woburn Abbey.

Passengers would take the train from Midland Line stations to Bedford where a coach would then take them to the park.

Then someone hit on the idea of getting some publicity for the promotion by bringing one of the park's residents to Nottingham by train where it would be photographed with the girls in the divisional office typing pool at Furlong House. The resident in question was to be a lion cub that would travel with its keeper from Bedford to Nottingham. There was then just the little problem of how to get lion and keeper to the divisional office in Furlong House about ½ a mile away from the station. Walking through the streets of Nottingham with a lion, even a young one on a lead, was not thought to be quite right. A volunteer with a car was needed.

So it was that the morning came when I found myself at Nottingham's Midland station with the task of transporting lion cub and keeper to Furlong House. Perhaps it was because of the film *Born Free* about a lioness and her cubs, but my image of lion cubs was of small, playful animals akin in size to a domestic cat. When the train from Bedford pulled in I soon got a rude awakening when an animal the size of a large dog emerged from the otherwise unoccupied guard's brake van (the guard had wisely settled himself in the van at the other end of the train) led by her keeper on a hefty chain. The 'cub' did not appear to have enjoyed the journey, as she moved her head from side to side accompanied by the occasional snarl.

We managed to negotiate the steps up to the ticket barrier and across the booking hall to where my Ford Cortina was parked. Now the lion cub had to be coaxed into the back of the vehicle. This was an interesting exercise as the car only had two doors, so the animal had to be pushed and pulled through the narrow gap behind the front seat. It was at this point that the keeper assured me she was really a very friendly lion and 'unlikely to bite'! Safely installed, our young lady filled the whole of the rear seat, and when I got into the driver's seat her fur brushed the back of my neck. Fortunately the business end of teeth and jaw were on the keeper's side of the car.

The couple of minutes' journey passed uneventfully and the lion cub was welcomed, from a respectful distance, by the staff at Furlong House. The photo shoot with the girls in the typing pool went to plan and a picture appeared in that evening's edition of the *Nottingham Post*. Job done! Memories of the day lingered, however, not least because of the all-pervading feline odour left in my car. But then it is not everyone who can say they have carried a lion in their car.

SOMETIMES ALMOST FICTION

——◁◦▷——

A posting to Glasgow provided David Barraclough with some quite dramatic new experiences

In the late spring of 1965 Eastern Region management considered that, after three years as goods agent at Boston, I should be moving on. I was directed to apply for positions, first as assistant goods agent at King's Cross and then as cartage manager at Bishopsgate. After three years as my own boss I resisted these moves to London, but I was promptly called for an interview by the assistant general manager and told, 'BR has paid for your traffic apprenticeship and you will go where you are told or the consequences could be severe.'

A week later I was instructed to report for interview for the job of utilisation officer in the Glasgow division. After 40 minutes Divisional Manager Jim Urquhart seemed satisfied and I was offered the job. With a staff of twenty-four I was responsible for the distribution and effective utilisation of all rolling stock, plus electric and diesel multiple units, and in addition to my team of inspectors I was involved in such other things as standards for carriage cleaning. This wide remit was to produce some situations that were unusual, to say the least.

I arrived in Glasgow a fortnight before the start of the Glasgow Fair Holidays when, to meet requirements for trains to English resorts, some 800 coaches had to be brought north to be cleaned and stored. When the exodus started the train guards would bring down the appropriate set from Polmadie yard to Glasgow Central station and unlock the doors on the platform side of the coaches. When, on one occasion, a platform change was made without anyone telling the guard all hell broke loose. Before a station announcement could be made suitcases were being used to smash windows and people were trying to join the train in any way they could. It proved a major task to get them out again, back to the concourse, and the damaged set replaced.

During the football season, special trains were run to distant games, the number being determined by police resources. For local games cheap fares were used to persuade volatile fans away from regular services, and local police would be advised of the routes and times of the trains carrying fans.

On a good day there would be few problems but it was not unknown for trains passing in opposite directions on the Edinburgh–Glasgow line to be stopped by use of the communication cord and for a battle to take place between the fans they carried.

During this period carriage-cleaning depots were staffed mainly by female cleaners who were very good at their job but very much a group to be reckoned with: cheerful, often boisterous and apt to treat outsiders with scant ceremony. In November 1966 when we closed Buchanan Street station, the station staff and carriage cleaners there were given the option of either redundancy or filling vacancies at the Cowlairs Carriage Sidings. All the Buchanan Street cleaners were men and those at Cowlairs mainly women, including women supervisors. The Buchanan Street foremen claimed that they should have priority for the Cowlairs positions but both management and unions rejected this idea. With this unwillingness to work under women supervisors it left only a few male cleaners to opt to go to Cowlairs and not one lasted more than six weeks there before resigning. Perhaps they were wise, for one of the Cowlairs cleaning supervisors was 'Big Margaret' whose word was absolute law. She was not afraid to resort to physical action to deal with any intransigence and was quite capable of lifting miscreants off their feet and shaking them into the proper path!

Working the traffic from the Ayrshire collieries was an intense and complex business with a steady flow of traffic passing over the colliery lines to reach the exchange sidings with the main line. On the main line south of Ayr were Maxwell and Bargany quarries, the latter involving an uphill haul to the exchange sidings and then Kilkerran Bank on the main line. The volume of traffic meant that it was frequently necessary to 'double the Bargany' (i.e. work the trains with a pair of locomotives), usually the 2-6-0 Horwich-built 'Crabs' which, working hard, tended to produce impressive pyrotechnics. In dry weather it was Control's practice to advise the Ayr fire brigade to stand by in readiness for any resultant lineside fires.

The 'Crabs' were splendid engines, both uphill and downhill, and with excellent brakes, which was a necessity when working in the Ayrshire coalfield. In the twilight years of steam Ayr Shedmaster Bennett did a splendid job of maintaining availability, sometimes even having to resort to using string (yes, really) to keeps parts of the locomotives in place. This excellent manager and master craftsman also managed to maintain the fleet of Swindon three-car DMU sets that worked the Ayrshire passenger services on just one line in the steam shed.

After steam was banished in 1967 we were given Type 2 diesel motive power, principally Class 25s supplemented by Clayton Type 1s south of the Clyde. The former were well received but the latter were 'utterly useless' and, to avoid lengthy delays due to failures, never let out on the line except in pairs – not infrequently three at a time had to be resorted too. North of the Clyde we had North British Type 2s returned from England on the basis of 'you made them, now make them work'. Gingerly they were tested on a variety of workings, one of which proved memorable.

The Scottish Region general manager laid on a two-day tour of the West Highland line in September for some VIPs, regional board members and two senior divisional managers. Using the general manager's saloon and a North British Type 2 diesel, the itinerary was off to Mallaig, then Fort William and Corpach Mill aluminium works and local distillery. The diesel failed just north of Rannoch and only just managed to struggle into the station loop, and that was that. Control was told by headquarters to use the diesel off the 4.30 p.m. sleeper service to King's Cross but refused to interfere with a revenue-earning service and sent a relief locomotive from Eastfield instead. The general manager's saloon was delayed for over 4 hours, but the entourage had an excellent high tea at the Rannoch Hotel and were not too upset. Next day came the blunt instruction, 'No North British Type 2s to venture on to the West Highland line.' Sometimes problems worked out well!

The occasional mishap sometimes had an unusual result. At 8.15 one morning there was some excitement in the Control office. A three-car DMU running empty from Shotts to West Calder to form a train to Edinburgh Waverley had struck a group of cattle that had strayed on to the line just short of Fauldhouse station. The resultant derailment saw the whole unit run up the platform ramp and come to rest upright and with no serious damage on the Up platform. Conveniently, it was not even fouling the running line to prevent other trains passing. It was, however, an interesting challenge for the breakdown train and crew.

Our liaison with the BTP was effective and ongoing. One example occurred at 4.50 one evening when the police rang Control wanting to close Strathbungo signal box in order to arrest the signalman on duty. The deputy chief controller pointed out the disruption this would cause to the evening peak-hour trains from Central and St Enoch stations. I asked the BTP inspector why the signalman was to be arrested and, after a moment's hesitation, was told that it was 'on suspicion of murder'. It was a serious, dramatic and difficult situation but we agreed on a course that would keep the box under close surveillance for the 1½ hours of the remaining shift and then move in for the arrest.

Theft was something of a problem in the Glasgow area. If a coal train was likely to be held up for more than a couple of hours we had to remove the wagon brasses before someone else did. Signalling and communications equipment was another vulnerable area. To combat thefts along the line we used a Signal & Telegraph (S&T) department gang in a Land Rover, carrying replacement equipment that could be deployed quickly to minimise train delays. However, after a time it became evident that there was a pattern in both location and modus operandi of the incidents. The BTP soon had the answer and were able to arrest our special S&T gang on duty and complete with their stolen material in the vehicle. The other shift gangs were warned and no more problems occurred.

My time at Glasgow proved challenging, interesting and rewarding. The passenger business (long distance and local) was substantial and backed by extensive carriage-stabling sidings and fifteen carriage-cleaning depots. In addition to the coal traffic we handled the output of five major steelworks, substantial business in export bricks in Palbrick wagons, iron ore to Ravenscraig, daily loads of explosives at Ardeer and Vanfits for the two Johnnie Walker bottling plants. Among the other important movements were the overnight deliveries of bread to Oban for onward conveyance to the Western Isles.

On the domestic front we lived on the third floor of a lovely, old stone tenement building where our doorbell at the entrance was still inscribed 'Servants'. Our milk was still being delivered by a horse-drawn milk float from which the milkman also offered hot breakfast rolls – something of an essential in Glasgow. Less pleasant was the violent tornado of October 1967 when dustbins and bricks went flying past our windows.

Before I left for Doncaster, my main sparring partner for three years, the leader of the Larkfield LDC, came to Hope Street to see me. This was the man who had once greeted me with the phrase 'this is war' and now said 'how glad he was to see the back of me'. But 'hard, but fair at all times' he acknowledged and we shook hands and wished each other well.

If you enjoyed this book, you may also be interested in …

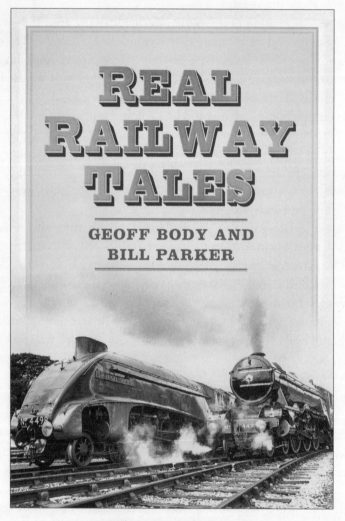

978 0 7509 5635 2